SALMON
FROM MARKET TO PLATE

when you want to eat salmon that
is good for you *and* the oceans

MAUREEN C. BERRY

Copyright 2016 Maureen C. Berry
Berry Publishing, Kentucky 42431
All rights reserved.
First edition published 2016.
Printed in the United States of America.

ISBN: 978-0-9973540-0-3

Library of Congress Control Number: 2016903974
Salmon From Market To Plate—when you want to eat salmon that is good for you and the oceans
1. Cooking
2. Reference

Photography by Maureen C. Berry
Book cover and interior design: Megan Johns
Editor: Katherine Pickett (POP Editorial Services)
Chef-Inspired Recipes and photographs reprinted by permission.
BAP logo reproduced by Steve Hedlund.
Wild Alaska salmon photography courtesy Mary Smith F/V Virga
Author's headshots by Rennan Quijano

For information about permission to reproduce any part of this book, including but not limited to, excerpts, photocopying, recipes, or any future means of reproducing text or images please contact the author at http://maureencberry.com.

Dedicated to my husband Larry, who encouraged me to put down the newspaper and start writing my dreams.

Heartfelt thanks to Victoria Allman, Chris DeVoto, Ron Duprat, Nora Galdiano, Rick Moonen, Martin Reed, True North Salmon, Verlasso Salmon, Alexander Weiss, and Virginia Willis for their recipes, generosity, and passion for sustainable fisheries and ocean conservation.

~M.C.B.

CONTENTS

PREFACE — XIII

INTRODUCTION — XIX

CHAPTER 1 WHAT IS SUSTAINABLE SALMON (AND WHY SHOULD YOU CARE)? — 1

CHAPTER 2 WILD SALMON — 11

CHAPTER 3 FARMED SALMON — 17

CHAPTER 4 BUYING SALMON — 27

CHAPTER 5 KITCHEN ESSENTIALS — 37

CHAPTER 6 COOKING SALMON — 50

CHAPTER 7 EVERYDAY SALMON RECIPES **57**

In the Oven

Slow-Roasted Salmon Salad: Three Ways **60**

Honey Mustard Salmon with Very Berry Vinaigrette **64**

Salmon Flatbread with Mandarin Orange and Fennel **67**

Salmon with Roasted Apples and Walnuts **69**

Cumin-Dusted Salmon Bowl with Peanut-Thai Slaw **72**

Slow Roasted Salmon with Blueberry Pan Sauce **76**

Salmon in Parchment **80**

On the Stove

Farmers Market Salmon Salad **86**

Salmon with Spicy Peach Salsa **90**

Summer Salmon Chowder **93**

Poached Salmon with Cheese Grits and Eggs **96**

Spicy Salmon Rice Bowl **99**

Salmon with Orange-Bourbon Glaze **101**

Simple Steamed Salmon **104**

Mediterranean Salmon with Chickpea Mash **106**

Salmon Corn Chowder **109**

Salmon Burger with Cranberry Yogurt **112**

Pan Grilled Salmon with Cilantro-Walnut Pesto **116**

On the Grill

Salmon with Pesto and Goat Cheese Crumbles 122

Grilled Salmon with Roasted Beets, Blue Cheese, and Pear Vinaigrette 125

CHAPTER 8 CHEF-INSPIRED RECIPES   129

Florida Sunshine Salmon with Avocado Mousse, Citrus Salsa, and Cilantro Oil *Chef Victoria Allman* 132

Baked Salmon with Bok Choy and Ginger *Twin Maples Organics Chefs Chris and Elizabeth Devoto* 137

Grilled Salmon with Cracked Pepper and Bacon *Chef Ron Duprat* 140

Salmon with Roasted Pepper, Kalamata, and Raisin Relish *Chef Nora Galdiano* 142

Grilled Salmon with Hoisin Glaze and Asian Slaw *Chef Rick Moonen* 145

Alaska King Lox *Blue Sea Labs Martin Reed* 148

Baked Shiitake-Tomato Atlantic Salmon *True North Salmon Company* 151

Baked Ancho Chile Verlasso Salmon Cakes with Lemon and Roasted Garlic Aioli *Verlasso Salmon* 153

Asian Glazed Grilled Salmon *MasterChef Junior Alexander Weiss* 157

Broiled Lemon Herb Salmon *Chef Virginia Willis* 160

ACKNOWLEDGMENTS	**165**
SHOPPING FOR SALMON	**168**
SUSTAINABLE ORGANIZATIONS AND RESOURCES	**170**
CONTRIBUTING CHEFS AND CORPORATIONS	**173**
INDEX	**176**
ABOUT THE AUTHOR	**181**

PREFACE

I grew up in Pittsburgh, Pennsylvania, surrounded by concrete and steel buildings, asphalt and chain-link-fenced school yards. In 1975 when I was fourteen, I saw the Atlantic Ocean for the first time while on a family vacation in Ocean City, Maryland. I fell in love immediately.

The briny wind crusted my face and whipped my curly, auburn hair into my eyes, making it difficult to brush later. Miles of white beach stretched as far as I could see. Each time my eyes searched the horizon, the deep blue sea tugged at my heart. I felt liberated.

That week in Ocean City, as I pushed my toes into the hot, gritty sand and considered how the blue color of my eyes matched the water, my fourteen-year-old soul bonded with the ocean. And like that, it became my muse. Its tides lured me; its pounding surf lulled me; its salty warm water nourished me; and it pulled at me like an undertow.

Midweek my uncles went crabbing. Not only was the word crabbing foreign to me, but so were the small blue live crustaceans brought home for steaming. My uncles pounded open the cooked crabs with wooden mallets on a newspaper-covered kitchen counter. I watched the adults through the salt-crusted glass sliding door of the back patio and was equally repulsed and awed by the aggressive smashing of the once blue, now bright red crabs. Mesmerized by their laughter, I watched my mom with her brothers and sisters pick the tiny pieces of meat from the crab with their hands. They plopped the butter-drenched, creamy white flesh into their mouths and swooned. My stomach grumbled. I craved that feeling of I-can't-get-enough, laughter-inducing eating.

For the remainder of the vacation, I watched the boats offshore and wondered if they too would return with crabs. I began to wonder about other creatures living in the ocean. While I continued to bodysurf and collect shells that week, I became more curious.

As I grew older and attended college in Pennsylvania, I couldn't get enough beach time. I took every opportunity to travel to various beaches along the East Coast: Virginia Beach, Rehoboth Beach, Atlantic City, Miami Beach. I dreamed of living near the ocean. When I saw the deep blue water, I became a different person, no longer the lonely, awkward kid from Pittsburgh but a confident, young woman who felt at peace and at home.

The ocean has a way of changing the lives of people who love it. I know. The ocean changed mine.

Just after my twenty-eighth birthday, I moved to Marathon, Florida, a tiny strip of land in the middle of the Florida Keys. I fulfilled my lifelong destiny to get away from the steel-and-concrete world of my youth. For ten years, I managed a sixty-four-seat run-down diner. Bacon and eggs, mullet and grits, deep-sea fishing for tuna, and backcountry bottom fishing for grouper and snapper filled my life. Food and fishing opened up an ocean of possibilities for my future. Life in the Florida Keys was where I discovered my love for all things seafood and ocean. While there, I cooked a variety of seafood. And lots of it.

I steamed, grilled, braised, fried, simmered, and sautéed white, flakey, tender-fleshed fish, such as grouper, snapper, mahi-mahi, wahoo, and sweet, succulent crabmeat. I learned how to make food look good. More importantly, I learned how to make food taste good.

It would be another decade, however, before I learned to love to eat fresh salmon.

After ten years managing the Marathon restaurant, my back, legs, and feet protested. I packed up my knives, flip-flops, and fishing rods and moved to Orlando, Florida.

For the next ten years, I sold groceries. First, to Walt Disney World for Sysco, then as a seafood broker in the wholesale distribution industry, showcasing products at trade shows and restaurants and to chefs. Finally, I found my niche as a seafood specialist, where I bought and sold fresh fish in the commodity fish world. *Seafood specialist* is a fancy term for someone who works ridiculously long hours in a refrigerated warehouse, selling cardboard boxes of dead fish packed in shaved ice. There is nothing glamorous about selling dead fish. But I wouldn't have it any other way. I loved my job.

I sold thousands of pounds of fresh salmon to chefs. I knocked on doors, made phone calls, and stood behind tables in convention halls. I did what I could to talk to people about buying salmon.

With an unlimited opportunity to cook and eat fresh seafood, I also loved to help people make the right decisions about what type of fish to buy.

One thing I knew for sure: of all the types of fish, chefs preferred to buy salmon.

And once I learned how to buy the "right" salmon and cook it properly, life quickly changed for me. I brought salmon home to bake, braise, fry, steam, and sear. I, too, preferred the sweet, buttery-rich, bold flavors of salmon. The chefs with whom I worked invited me to eat at their restaurants, where I learned simple cooking techniques and delicious recipes for preparing the salmon I sold them. I became confident in how to pair flavors to the distinct, rich flavor of salmon.

During this same period, I learned some people want to eat salmon but are afraid of it. They don't know what to buy, how to cook it, or what to do with it once it is cooked. So they avoid it.

Does this sound like you?

Don't worry. Once upon a time, I was that person. Remember, not only did I grow up far away from the ocean, but for years I also never ate salmon. My early experiences with seafood were limited to tuna noodle casserole, McDonald's fish sandwiches, Mrs. Paul's fish sticks on Friday, and fried cod and scallop pieces, an occasional giveaway from the chefs at the corner Italian restaurant in my neighborhood.

So come with me and we'll take an I-can't-get-enough, laughter-inducing, salmon-eating journey together. With *Salmon*, I will show you how to buy, cook, eat, and love salmon, too.

INTRODUCTION

Nutritionists, doctors, and medical experts agree, eating salmon has a long list of benefits. In addition to high levels of omega-3 fatty acids and anti-inflammatory properties, salmon is a terrific source of lean protein. Still, people shy away despite the prevailing knowledge it is good for you.

Over the years, one of the most common statements I have heard is, "I love to eat fish, but I don't want to cook it." My response has always been the same. My head tilts to the right, my brows furrow, and my eyes wander around a bit. Then I ask, "Why?"

You see, cooking salmon, or any fish for that matter is one of the easiest things to do. With a little knowledge about which species to buy, how to shop, and which kitchen tools to use, you will soon become a salmon-cooking and -eating phenom. Once you get over your fear of the unknown, you will master my easy-to-prepare salmon recipes and cooking techniques and will love to cook and eat salmon just as much as I do.

During the many years I worked in the food industry, I learned a few things, a list of sorts, about what makes people afraid of salmon. Let's see if you can find a little of yourself in my list.

First, maybe you've never bought fish before. You don't know how to order it at the seafood counter and you're afraid of embarrassing yourself, or worse, buying the wrong piece of fish. This is a category of food you know nothing about and you need a point of entry.

Second, maybe you're unsure about which type of salmon to buy. After all, there are many salmon species and types on the market: wild or farm-raised, king or sockeye, fresh, frozen, and canned. Throw in the latest catchphrase, "sustainable seafood," and it's no wonder shoppers are confused.

Third, salmon has a distinct flavor, decidedly different than white, flakey cod, grouper, halibut, or snapper—and that can make it intimidating to those new to eating fish. If you don't cook it properly or prepare it with the right ingredients, will your fresh, healthful salmon dinner turn into an expensive disaster? And let's face it. Sometimes the seafood department has a not so pleasant fishy odor to it. The last thing you want is that smell in your kitchen.

And fourth, salmon is orange or some shade of reddish orange or pinkish orange, which some diners find disconcerting. Do you shy away from salmon because of its color? When I see the orange color of salmon I think of health and nutrition. I think of sweet, juicy, plump oranges; crunchy carrots; dense, rich pumpkin pie; the flesh of butternut squash and papaya, and I can't wait to dig in. But if you aren't familiar with salmon, the unusual color may add to the mystery.

Others of you may already know you want to eat more salmon—you hear it is delicious and easy to make, and you want to get all those heart-healthy omega-3s you keep reading about—yet you never buy it when you shop for groceries. I suspect there are a few reasons for that. Let's see if I can find one or two that fit your lifestyle and buying habits:

- You are confused about the different kinds of salmon.
  _____

- You don't know how much to buy.
  _____

- You don't know how to prepare it.

- The seafood department smells funny.

- You live nowhere near the ocean.

All valid reasons for not buying and cooking salmon. With *Salmon*, however, I eliminate every one of those concerns.

Now one more factor keeps some people from eating salmon on a regular basis. Many people I have talked to say they consider fresh fish and seafood a celebratory meal. They eat salmon when they go out for their anniversary or at a wedding, and they have a hard time meeting those standards in their own kitchen. Maybe that's you. But maybe, just maybe, you want to learn to make restaurant-quality salmon dishes, save money and impress your family and friends. *Salmon* is going to show you how to do just that.

Here's what you can expect.

Seafood sustainability is important for several reasons. In What Is Sustainable Salmon (and Why Should You Care)? I define *sustainability* and show how it affects you, your family, the environment, and the future.

In two short chapters, Wild Salmon and Farmed Salmon, I define and compare the differences between wild and farmed salmon to help get you up to speed on your buying choices. Then, in Buying Salmon, I offer simple, easy-to-remember tips and shopping guidelines for when you're at the market. You'll learn to make sustainable choices when you shop.

In Kitchen Essentials, you will stock your shelves with spices, seasonings, oils, and more so you have the essential ingredients to create easy, delicious salmon recipes every day of the week. Also, you will learn about the basic, everyday kitchen equipment and tools that make these salmon recipes work.

One of the most important chapters, Cooking Salmon, wraps up all you've ingested so far with a discussion of three simple cooking methods: In The Oven, On The Stove and On The Grill. With this foundation, you will be ready to dive into the first recipe.

In Everyday Salmon Recipes, I offer twenty easy-to-prepare recipes. These recipes don't require a culinary degree or top-of-the-line restaurant equipment. They are delicious and accessible to any cook who wants to learn. Here you will find quick and easy midweek dinners as well as luxurious weekend fare.

In the final chapter, Chef-Inspired Salmon Recipes, I share ten salmon recipes contributed by chefs who support sustainable seafood practices and ocean conservation. These recipes are for cooks looking to up their game with more complex, incredible flavors.

Once you learn the basic cooking techniques, you will be on your way to developing your own salmon recipes with confidence. The information in *Salmon* is designed to help you become a salmon lover long before you prepare and cook the first recipe and beyond your last cooked salmon meal. In the end, your buying, cooking, and eating of salmon will be determined by your own creativity, schedule, cooking tools, and budget. No more fear!

The more you know about something, the more you can open up your heart to love it. Whether you buy fresh wild Alaska sockeye salmon or sustainably farm-raised Atlantic salmon; prepare one salmon recipe once a month, twice a week, or by the seasons, I hope *Salmon* inspires you to eat more delicious, heart-healthy salmon all year long.

1
WHAT IS SUSTAINABLE SALMON
AND WHY SHOULD YOU CARE?

> "IN THE END, WE WILL CONSERVE ONLY WHAT WE LOVE; WE WILL LOVE ONLY WHAT WE UNDERSTAND; AND WE WILL UNDERSTAND ONLY WHAT WE ARE TAUGHT."
>
> — BABA DIOUM, SENEGALESE CONSERVATIONIST

Sustainable has become a popular word in a variety of contexts and because of that, it is often misunderstood. The easiest way to describe it is this: a sustainable product is one that can be used without being destroyed or destroying the environment. Add *salmon* to the equation—a living organism that we plan to eat—and things get a little murky. How can we eat something and not destroy it or its environment, the ocean? To understand the concept, we have to think more broadly than one fish. Simply put, sustainable salmon refers to those fish that are caught or raised in a manner that doesn't harm the environment and will provide salmon for future generations.

Now consider the following two expanded explanations of what *sustainable salmon* means. One presents simple, appetizer-sized definitions; the other is the main course.

THE APPETIZER

The National Oceanic and Atmospheric Administration (NOAA), the federal agency dedicated to the science of the oceans and atmosphere, states, "Seafood is sustainable when the fishery it was harvested from is managed in a way that sustains the use of the fishery and marine ecosystem for future generations."

According to Sea Choice, a nonprofit organization dedicated to making smart seafood decisions for healthy oceans tomorrow, *sustainable seafood* is defined as "fish or shellfish that is caught or farmed in ways that consider the long-term viability of harvested populations and the oceans' health and ecological integrity."

THE MAIN COURSE

Those two definitions from NOAA and Sea Choice lay the groundwork for our understanding, but there is more to it than simple definitions can convey. Sustainable salmon can be likened to a four-prong fork where each tine represents a point of responsibility: fishermen, conservationists, governments, and consumers.

- Fishermen work to support their lifestyles and supply a product (salmon).

- Conservationists work to protect the ecology and environment.

- Governments create fishing guidelines and regulations to reduce illegal fishing practices, preserve fisheries, and protect consumers.

- And consumers are tasked with learning what to buy at the market.

Like a fork, each tine has to be doing its part in order for the system to be successful.

THE FISHERMAN

Wild Alaska salmon fishing is an ancient practice with significant cultural and historical heritage. However, in recent history, the eating public's desire for buttery, rich-tasting salmon exploded, and soon, the global demand outstripped the supply. To solve this challenge, aquaculture, or farmed salmon, came into vogue in the United States in the 1950s. Notably, this innovation in fishing did not begin in the United States. Rather, the rich and diverse history of aquaculture dates back several millennia. Yet, the industry has been fraught with problems of low product-quality standards. It wasn't until recent advances in technology allowed for greater quality control that the aquaculture industry matured into what it is today (although in many farms, consistent quality continues to be an issue).

> Whether fishermen practice safe fishing methods in the wild or in a controlled environment, the takeaway is that the fishing practice shouldn't harm the environment, the health of the fish population, the ocean's ecosystems, or the consumer.

For instance, in a commercial fishing business in Alaska, boats are equipped with specific gear and observers to help eliminate bycatch, the term used to indicate all the species of seafood that are caught during the fishing process that are not among the targeted fish. In the Alaska groundfish fisheries, which target cod, haddock, pollock, and flounder, Chinook salmon are a part of the bycatch. Bycatch is a serious problem in the seafood industry, not just in the salmon industry. Those fish that are unintentionally pulled from the water are not simply thrown back to fight and live another day. Although some fish are when harvested by fishers who practice sustainable fishing methods. However, many fish are mortally wounded and then discarded. The result? A negative impact on the ecosystem. The goal of a sustainable fishery and responsible fishermen is to reduce, and ultimately avoid bycatch. Some say it is a lofty goal. I say let us dream about salmon for the future.

Another way fishermen are working to create a sustainable environment has taken hold at the grassroots level, where fishermen provide accountability and traceability. In some regions of the United States and in fish farms, fish have a bar-code tag. Using QR technology, consumers can scan the tag on the fish with their phone to learn where and when the fish was caught, the name of the boat, and in some instances, the boat captain. Small- and large-scale fishermen work with retail and wholesale markets to adopt sustainable seafood policies to bring fresh, sustainably sourced salmon to the market.

Lastly, Community Supported Fishery (CSF) programs are popping up around the globe. A CSF offers consumers a weekly share of fresh seafood for a pre-paid fee, modeled after the popular Community Supported Agriculture (CSA) programs. A CSF helps support local economies, fishermen, and the oceans while providing you the consumer, with fresh, sustainable fish.

THE CONSERVATIONIST

Numerous conservation organizations work independently and together to create sustainable seafood campaigns to preserve the oceans and support a safe, long-term supply of seafood. The goals of these campaigns are to create sustainable, responsible fisheries, safe working environments for fishermen, and less illegal fishing and bycatch. NOAA Fisheries defines bycatch as "discarded catch of any living marine resource, plus unobserved mortality due to a direct encounter with fishing gear." The shared vision of these organizations is to keep the oceans and fish populations healthy and to produce healthy, sustainable seafood to sell at the market for generations to come.

Independent organizations like Monterey Bay Aquarium work to educate consumers. In 1999, the aquarium created Seafood Watch, a science-based sustainable seafood recommendation program. Seafood Watch is the gold standard in ocean conservation and sustainable seafood. Available as downloads or as a mobile app, the Seafood Watch "pocket guides" are color-coded, making buying decisions easy to understand.

Operating out of Stony Brook, New York, The Safina Center (formerly Blue Ocean Institute) is a science- and art-based institution with a focus on seafood and the oceans. It is another gold-star organization in the campaign to protect and conserve seafood fisheries. Since 2003, its focus has been on ocean challenges and what that means to the ecosystem and population, helping consumers make better choices through books, television, and public speaking.

There are numerous third-party organizations that certify a fishery to make sure its practices and methods don't destroy habitats, have a negative impact on the fish and oceans, or otherwise harm the environment. Two prominent global seafood certification organizations are the Marine Stewardship Council (MSC) and Best Aquatic Practice (BAP). Both encourage best fishing and farming practices. Look for the blue, oval MSC label and the round, blue BAP label when you shop for salmon. Download the mobile apps to learn more.

THE GOVERNMENT

It is not enough to have dedicated fishermen and organizations working to support the effort for sustainable seafood populations. Without government regulation, the ocean's fisheries and the world's farmed fisheries would exploit the current fish and seafood populations, and if unchecked, their practices would ultimately lead to extinction.

Two important measures that the US government has taken to protect the future of seafood are periodic closures and catch shares in certain areas of the United States. Catch shares allot individual fishermen, communities, and fisheries with a certain number of fish that can be harvested. Periodic closures allow for the regrowth of a population. Together, these measures can help ensure sustainability. Although not foolproof, both practices have worked in several fisheries, including salmon fisheries, with promise for more fisheries to follow.

In addition, salmon aquaculture has made significant improvements over the past few decades with regard to feed ratio, methods of farming, and impact on the environment, which is largely determined by the method of farming. The best methods of aquaculture include closed containment, which safeguards the natural environment from the pollution and disease transfer associated with fish farms. Highlighted in Chapter 3 are two examples of successful, sustainably farmed salmon operations.

As you can see, protecting the safety and future of sustainable salmon, both wild and farmed, is both simple and complex. Sustainable salmon is not just about fishermen, conservationists, eco-labels, and government regulators, however; it also involves you, the consumer.

THE CONSUMER

Sustainable salmon is the future—*your* future. When you become aware of the issues of the salmon industry and the challenges of an unchecked, unregulated ocean and ecosystem, you can become a sustainable salmon steward. When you know how sustainable salmon regulations and actions influence the future of the oceans and fish populations, you make better choices at the market. In simple terms, buying sustainable salmon means you care about your health, your children, your grandchildren and their grandchildren, the economy, ecology, and the future of the oceans. While that may feel like a burden, it is an undeniable fact: we live in a closed system in which our choices make all the difference for all of us, everywhere.

The world population is expected to grow to nine billion by 2050. With that growth comes the demand for protein. Since salmon is an excellent source of protein, omega-3s, vitamins, and minerals, and it tastes great, the demand for more salmon will increase with the expanding population. Both wild salmon and farmed salmon are needed for a sustainable future.

Buying, cooking, and eating sustainable salmon can make a big difference in your life and in the world around you. Your purchasing habits are a choice and a responsibility. When you choose to buy wild Alaska salmon or sustainably farmed salmon, you become a sustainable salmon rock star, helping to save the oceans and leave the planet a healthier place.

Now that you are caught up on the sustainable salmon basics, let's look at the differences between wild and farmed salmon.

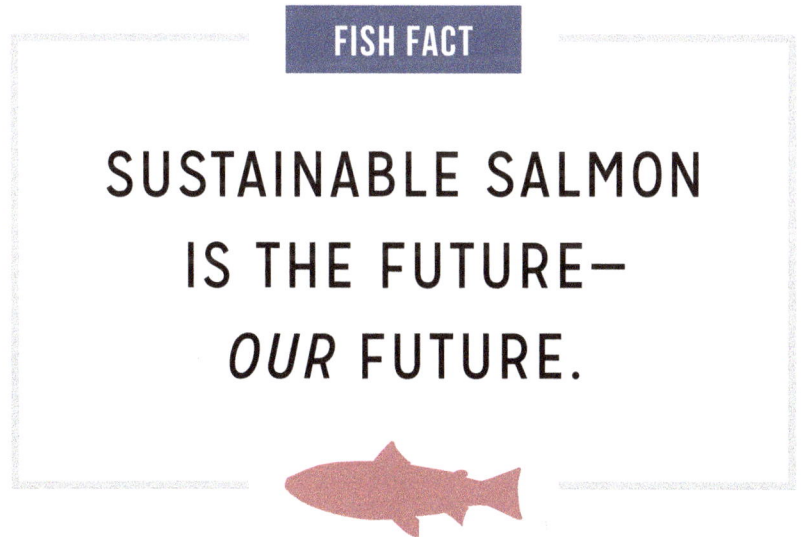

FISH FACT

SUSTAINABLE SALMON IS THE FUTURE— *OUR* FUTURE.

2
WILD SALMON

At one time in the United States, wild salmon was available from the North Atlantic Ocean as well as the Pacific Ocean and Alaska. Today, because of overfishing, Atlantic salmon runs are virtually gone, with only remnants surviving in 11 rivers, according to NOAA Fisheries. Nearly all wild salmon consumed in the United States today comes from Alaska and the Pacific Ocean.

Here are a few more wild salmon facts:

- Wild salmon is available year-round in the United States.

- The active fishing season in Alaska and the Pacific Ocean for wild salmon is May through September.

- Salmon purchased out of season is either frozen or previously frozen (PF) fish. PF fish has been caught, cleaned, portioned, and then frozen at sea or in a fish-processing facility before shipment to the grocer. The grocer then thaws the fish before displaying it in the case for sale and labeling it accordingly.

- Wild salmon range in size from five pounds to more than twenty pounds.

- Salmon gets its distinctive flavor and color range—from pale pink to orange to red—from the food it eats, much the way oysters' flavor comes from the soil in which they live.

Five species of Alaska salmon are commercially available throughout the year, but the season for fresh fish is just five months long. King salmon marks the beginning of the fishing season each May, and pink salmon ends the season in September. The following list presents the species in the order in which they are harvested throughout the season.

KING
also called chinook

The largest of the Alaska salmon species, king salmon has a full flavor and a reddish-orange color. The fillets can be several inches thick in their center. This is the "king" of all salmon, named so for its size, superior oil content, and full flavor. White-tablecloth restaurants serve king salmon. Expect to pay a premium price for king salmon whether you buy whole, fillet, steak, or smoked.

SOCKEYE
also called red

The Alaska salmon with the deepest red appearance, sockeye has a rich flavor and high oil content. The smaller size and bold color of sockeye are prized in markets and kitchens around the world.

COHO
also called silver

Its orange-red color, rich texture, and mild flavor make coho an attractive salmon for both restaurants and retail markets. I call it the workhorse of salmon.

KETA
also called chum

Keta has a delicate flavor. It is light orange and medium-size, with lower oil content. It is an excellent choice for smoking, steaks, and slow roasting.

PINK

also called humpy

This salmon species is the most prevalent salmon on the market. It is the least expensive due to its abundance. Pink salmon is a pale orange-pink. It is a small fish, and its oil content is lowest of all the Alaska salmon species. Pink salmon is sold smoked, canned, and in fillets.

Keep in mind, in many areas of the United States, fresh wild Alaska salmon is not available at the market. In these regions, your best option for sustainable wild Alaska salmon is the freezer aisle. To be sure you are buying sustainable salmon, read the label. Look for the logos and names of trusted organizations like Alaska Seafood Marketing Institute (ASMI), MSC, BAP, and for terms such as "domestic," "sustainable," or "caught in the USA/Alaska." Lastly, ask your grocer to bring Alaska salmon to your market.

3

FARMED SALMON

Historically, salmon farms were not regulated, resulting in contamination and disease. The fish feed was poorly managed, which led to overfishing of the wild fish species used to make the fish feed.

But all that is changing for the better. And just in time, too, because according to the World Wildlife Fund (WWF), farmed salmon accounts for 70 percent of salmon on the market. That number will grow as the global population expands and demands more protein. WWF also states, "Over 85 percent of marine fish stocks are considered either fully exploited or overfished, and more than one in five fisheries has collapsed."

Here are a few facts you should know about farmed salmon:

- Aquaculture has a history dating back millennia, though its exact origins are unknown. Farmed salmon, a form of aquaculture, has been around in the US since the 1950s.

- The farmed salmon industry has grown exponentially since its advent to provide much-needed protein for the growing global community.

- Farmed salmon is available year-round.

- The size and color of farmed salmon are uniform. An average farmed salmon fillet is four to five pounds, and its color is orange. It is labeled Atlantic farmed salmon, or PF Atlantic salmon.

- Farmed salmon costs less than most wild salmon on the market.

- Farmed salmon is raised in pens, tanks, and controlled environments. These environments may be an ocean pen, a

> **OVER 85 PERCENT OF MARINE FISH STOCKS ARE CONSIDERED EITHER FULLY EXPLOITED OR OVERFISHED, AND MORE THAN ONE IN FIVE FISHERIES HAS COLLAPSED.**

— WORLD WILDLIFE FUND (WWF)

manufactured stream, or a hatchery. Traditional farmed salmon are fed a combination of fishmeal, fish oil, and wild fish.

FEEDING FARMED SALMON

Two challenges face the farmed salmon industry in regards to feed: the amount of feed required to raise farmed salmon and the ingredients of the feed. Both have implications for sustainability.

Feed conversion ratios, also called fish in–fish out, estimate how many pounds of food are required to raise one pound of fish. For farmed salmon that ratio was 10:1 in the 1950s. In todays' market, it is 4:1. To show scale, other farmed animals such as cows, chickens, and pigs have much higher feed conversion ratios. Beef ratios can range from six to 25 pounds of feed to produce one pound of meat, depending on whether the cattle are fed corn or grass. The average ratio for pork is 4:1, and for chicken, 2:1. The ratio goal for maximum benefit is 1:1. At 4:1, salmon has an efficient feed ratio and it is expected to improve in the future.

Why is this important? Besides the economic implications for the farmers, an efficient feed conversion ratio means less impact on the fish populations that are used to feed the farmed fish.

Although the feed ratio for salmon is now in line with that of other farmed animals, there is still the matter of what the salmon are being fed. What ingredients make up the farmed salmon diet that makes it *not* sustainable? Two words: wild fish.

According to the WWF, "Aquaculture is contributing to overfishing through the use of wild caught fish as feed for farmed fish." Those seafood species used for salmon food—anchovies, pilchards, mackerel, herring, and whiting—are being removed from the oceans faster than the fish are able to reproduce, causing a significant and potentially irreversible depletion of these fish populations. The result is a negative environmental impact for fish populations and the ecology of the oceans.

However, scientists and other experts agree that aquaculture is necessary to feed the world's growing protein demands and to protect the ocean's population. It is imperative that the farmed salmon industry continues on its trend to reduce the fish feed ratio and find alternative solutions to make fish feed more sustainable. Fortunately, change is already occurring. And all farmed salmon are not raised equally.

One company that raises sustainably farmed salmon is Verlasso Salmon, an aquaculture production facility in Chile. The feed conversion ratio for Verlasso Salmon is 1:1. How does VS do that? The company replaces the fish oil in the feed with yeast to produce omega-3 fatty acids, the heart-healthy ingredient in salmon. For its overall sustainability, the ocean-raised farmed salmon from VS is rated a "good alternative" by Monterey Bay Aquarium's Seafood Watch program, the gold standard in ocean conservation.

Another sustainable aquaculture facility in North America is True North Salmon Company. Raised in a natural environment along the coast of Maine and Canada, True North salmon is free of dyes, antibiotics and growth hormones. Its feed conversion ratio is 1.2 kilograms of feed per 1 kilogram of fish produced.

In regard to advancements on fish feed, two feed manufactures, Aurora Algae and Fycology, use algae powder to replace some of the wild fish stocks in their fish feed.

If your market doesn't sell Verlasso Salmon or True North Salmon, ask the store manager to bring salmon in that is independently certified by a third party organization like Marine Stewardship Council (MSC) or Best Aquaculture Practices (BAP). Use your cold hard cash to help the future of our growing global population and the oceans.

Use your cold hard cash to help the future of our growing global population and the oceans.

AQUACULTURE SAFETY AND STANDARDS

To make the practice of raising farmed salmon safer, the Global Aquaculture Alliance (GAA) created its first certification process, called Best Aquaculture Practices (BAP). Since 1997, GAA, a nonprofit nongovernmental organization, has been dedicated to advancing environmentally and socially responsible aquaculture. There are more than 179 BAP-certified salmon farms around the globe. That number will continue to grow.

BAP regulates aquaculture facilities the same way MSC monitors wild fisheries. BAP's compliance requirements focus on water quality, feed ratios, ecological impacts, work environments, animal welfare, sea lice containment, and traceability, which means knowing where the fish come from, to create socially responsible and environmentally friendly salmon.

You may have heard talk in the news over the years regarding these compliance areas. In particular, fish escapement and sea lice are often used as fodder for the media because these challenges can have a significant impact on the wider environment. Poor compliance with these two factors has given aquaculture a bad rap.

The problem arises when farmed salmon escape from their pens, whether through a hole in the net caused by a boat or a large predator, wear and tear, or human error. In the event of an escape, farmed salmon compete with wild salmon for food and habitat and may spread disease such as sea lice.

I know firsthand about sea lice. In 2008 when I worked for the wholesale distributor in Florida, I sold thousands and thousands of pounds of farmed salmon to the restaurant industry. In fact, one account bought 95 percent of the salmon I purchased from one aquaculture salmon fishery in Chile.

The aquaculture fishery I worked with had an environmental problem. The salmon developed infectious salmon anemia (ISA), a farmed salmon disease commonly spread by sea lice. The disease reached outbreak proportions and the fishery closed its pens. I bought salmon from another farmed area, but because this issue had a direct effect on me and my clients, I became aware and concerned about the issues of farmed salmon.

In the weeks that followed the closures, one question began to bother me. If farmed salmon was so bad to eat and so destructive for the environment, I wondered, why were so many people eating farmed salmon instead of wild salmon?

So I made a few calls to the fisheries on the West Coast. I learned how supply and demand contributes to the need for aquaculture in the US. Sadly for Americans, the majority of wild Alaska salmon is exported.

> Without farmed salmon, the consumer demand in the US could not be met.

NOW, SHOULD *YOU* EAT FARMED SALMON?

Ultimately, that is a personal decision, and you must consider the benefits and risks for yourself. Health experts believe the benefits of eating farmed salmon outweigh the risks. Exceptions are pregnant and nursing women and children. Ecologists' beliefs will vary depending on whether they are proponents of farmed salmon or not. Moderation is key when you are unsure of the origins of the farmed salmon.

However, if you are still on the fence about whether to eat farmed salmon, I offer these thoughts and suggestions:

 Aquaculture is changing for the better with regard to certification, accountability, traceability, and production of more sustainable fish feed.

 Several methods of developing feed for farmed fish are evolving. Companies on the forefront of change for fish feed are Verlasso Salmon, Aurora Algae, and Fycology. Eating a variety of seafood species as well as a mix of wild salmon, sustainably sourced farmed salmon, and BAP-certified salmon decreases the risks associated with eating farmed salmon alone.

With time and technological advances, aquaculture practices and salmon farms of the future will produce more sustainable salmon. Again, moderation is the key to eating a sustainable salmon diet. Develop a meal plan that is healthy for both you and the oceans, one that ensures the likelihood of healthy seafood for future generations.

Are you ready to shop for salmon?

4
BUYING SALMON

Regardless of the type of salmon you buy, or where you buy it, by law, all salmon sold in the United States must be labeled. Labels identify the species, country of origin, and whether the salmon is farmed, frozen, frozen at sea, previously frozen, wild, or a combination of these designations.

To make your salmon shopping experience easier, shop at sustainably conscious markets.

> Look for labels from conservation groups on the salmon, a sign the market supports sustainable fishermen and practices that promote traceability, transparency, and accountability.

One rating system, Seafood Watch, Monterey Bay Aquarium's sustainable seafood program, offers a simple color-coded rating system. Green indicates the best choice for sustainability, yellow means the fish is a good alternative, and red indicates those fish that should be avoided.

With technological advances and improved fisheries management, seafood labeling evolves. Fish populations become healthier and less overfished meaning a seafood species can go from "good alternative" to "best choice" as a result of these practices. Conversely, salmon labeled "best choice" today may be on the yellow list in the future because of an unregulated fishery or a host of other factors.

Other organizations have also developed conservation programs and seafood rating systems to help make shopping easier. These systems make the seafood industry safer, more accountable, and healthier for the future of fish, the oceans, and you. Three organizations in particular have made significant contributions to these efforts. The Safina Center (formerly Blue Ocean Institute), a science-based organization, created its rating program, Seafood Choices, to help consumers buy sustainable seafood. Global Aquaculture Alliance offers its blue BAP label, and Marine Stewardship Council (MSC) has developed its blue oval label and a mobile app to help make buying farmed salmon easier.

Several retailers in the United States known to support the sustainable seafood movement include, but are not limited to, Giant Eagle, Harris Teeter, Whole Foods Market, The Fresh Market, Trader Joe's, Costco, Target, Weis Markets, Sprouts Family Markets, Wegmans, and Walmart. Ask your market about its sustainable seafood program.

You don't know what to ask, you say? These five questions will help you to become a savvy, sustainable salmon shopper:

FISHY QUESTIONS TO ASK

1. WHERE DOES THAT SALMON COME FROM?
2. IS IT WILD OR FARM-RAISED?
3. HOW IS THE FISH CAUGHT?
4. CAN I SMELL THAT FISH?
5. WHAT DAYS DOES THE SEAFOOD DEPARTMENT RECEIVE ITS FISH?

Get to know the people behind the counter who sell the fish. Are they trustworthy and reliable with their information? Are they willing to help you find the answers to your questions? They may not have the answers to your questions immediately, so be patient, but persistent. Or continue looking for a seafood market until you find one that you can trust.

On November 19, 2015, the U.S. FDA approved AquAdvantage salmon, a genetically modified (GM) farmed salmon. AquAdvantage salmon is engineered to grow faster, is safe to eat, and is as nutritious as a non-engineered salmon, according to the FDA. The extensive study also established that AquAdvantage salmon will not have a negative impact on the environment since the salmon will be grown in land-based facilities in Panama and Canada, making it "extremely unlikely that the fish could escape and establish themselves in the wild," according to fda.gov. Escapement into the wild is just one of the concerns against raising salmon in open ocean pens.

Additionally, GM salmon, also called "Frankenfish" by critics, does not have to be labeled as such by law. However, it could be a few years before it is available in your market. To learn more about how GM salmon is produced, contact the manufacturer, AquaBounty Technologies.

HOW TO BECOME A SALMON-BUYING ROCK STAR

Buying, cooking, and eating sustainable salmon is a choice—*your* choice. When you choose to buy sustainably sourced salmon, you are a responsible, "sustainable" seafood consumer. Whether you choose to buy fresh or frozen, farmed or wild, if you keep the following ten tips in mind, you'll be on your way to becoming a smart, sustainable salmon shopper.

Ten Tips for Buying Fresh Salmon

1. Buy fresh salmon the same day, or the day before, you are going to cook.

2. Buy four to six ounces of salmon per serving.

3. Bring an insulated bag to transport the salmon home and either ask for a small bag of ice or bring your own to keep the fish cool. A frozen gel pack will also work.

4. When you shop, buy salmon last. This is especially important if you forgot your cooler bag.

5. Ask your fishmonger where your salmon is from if it is not labeled. (It should be labeled, but not all stores follow this mandate.) Don't be afraid to ask how it was fished. You may not get an answer right away, but the more you ask, the better chance the retailer will find the answer for you.

6. Point to the exact piece you want. It should be bright, firm, and evenly colored, not dry or falling apart (two signs the salmon is old). After it is weighed, before it is wrapped up, say, "I'd like to smell that." It should smell mild, clean, and like the ocean. Salmon that doesn't smell good in the store will not smell any better when you get it home.

7. If you are suspicious about the way the salmon smells, ask for another piece; or ask which day the store receives its salmon shipments, and schedule your salmon buying for those days.

Conversely, if you don't like the way any of the fresh salmon looks at the counter, head to the freezer aisle.

8. Ask the fishmonger to portion the fish and remove the skin (if you prefer) and pin bones, unless you're really good with a knife and tweezers. Often the bones are already removed.

9. When you get home, keep the salmon in its original package in the coldest part of your refrigerator (this is usually the back of a shelf) until you are ready to cook for up to two days. If you will not be cooking the day you buy, or the next, freeze it immediately for up to three months. Freezing salmon is the best way to keep it fresh.

10. When you remove the salmon from the refrigerator and take it out of its packaging, please, please, please remember to take out the trash the same night you cook the salmon. Or place the packaging in an airtight bag in the freezer until your next scheduled garbage service. Don't forget! You will thank me later.

You may not find fresh salmon in your market. This is where frozen salmon is your best friend. Often frozen salmon is the best sustainably sourced salmon at the market. While not all markets offer wild frozen salmon, it is becoming more common throughout the country, even in rural parts of the United States. Ask your market to bring in frozen wild Alaska salmon.

Five Tips for Buying Frozen Salmon

1. Make sure the seal is not broken on the vacuum pack.

2. Check for signs of frostbite or ice crystals, a sign the fish has been frozen, thawed, and refrozen. (Yes, it happens!)

3. Read the labels on the package. Look for the words "caught in Alaska," "sustainably sourced," "domestic," or "caught in America."

4. Look for and familiarize yourself with certification labels such as the oval blue MSC label, the ASMI label, the round blue BAP label, and others mentioned in this book.

5. And don't forget, thaw frozen fish in the refrigerator 24 hours before you plan to cook.

Up to this point, I have assumed you buy your salmon at the grocery store or from a local fish market. However, if your grocery store does stock sustainably farmed salmon or wild Alaska salmon, or you live nowhere near a trustworthy fish market, you have a few alternatives.

Buying salmon online is fast and easy. With a few clicks, you can have fresh, frozen, or previously frozen salmon at your doorstep the next day. Be prepared to pay for overnight shipping, though, and be aware some vendors require a minimum order in weight to keep the freight cost down. If you decide you want to go this route but hail from a family of two, consider inviting your salmon-loving family, friends, or colleagues to pitch in to share the cost.

Another option is to buy your salmon directly from the boat, or a consortium of boats in a community supported fishery (CSF). Again, a

CSF is similar to a community-supported agriculture (CSA) where you buy a "share" from a small-scale farmer or fisherman. These men and women use sustainable fishing methods, which help reduce bycatch and protect the oceans' valuable resources, to bring you fresh, premium salmon. Each share buys a predetermined amount of fish during the fishing season. While the cost of salmon may be higher in a CSF, you will know when, where, how, and who caught your salmon, from boat-to-plate. Some CSFs only have pickup destinations and do not ship. For more information on salmon-buying recommendations, check the Shopping for Salmon section in the back of this book.

It's not enough to know how to buy salmon. Once you get it home you have to know how to cook it. Cooking salmon successfully means not just knowing how to read a recipe but also having the right ingredients and kitchen tools. In the next chapter we'll look at what pantry essentials you'll need and which pots, pans, utensils, and gadgets can help you become a successful salmon-loving cook.

5
KITCHEN ESSENTIALS

One obstacle that makes cooking an unfamiliar product harder is not having the right ingredients or the right kitchen equipment to make the recipe. I have great news. When it comes to cooking salmon, less is better.

STOCKING YOUR KITCHEN

You'll need these three essential ingredients to make your recipes rock:

THE ESSENTIALS

OILS: CANOLA, GRAPESEED, OLIVE, SAFFLOWER

———

KOSHER SALT

———

BLACK PEPPER, WHOLE WITH A GRINDER (PREFERABLE)

How simple is that?

Many other ingredients are interchangeable. Take citrus. Don't have a lemon? Use lime or orange. Yes, orange flavor is different from lemon, but what is important is the reaction of the acid in the citrus to the salmon.

> **Don't be afraid to play and experiment with your food until you find what you like.**

You may not enjoy some of the common ingredients in salmon recipes, such as ginger, wasabi, or honey. You do not need them to make great-tasting salmon, but you do need good-quality oils, salt, and pepper. When a recipe calls for wine, use a dry white wine. Here's The Golden Rule: if you wouldn't drink the wine, then don't cook with it.

The following box contains some of the ingredients I always reach for when I cook salmon. Buy what you can afford. And remember, this list is not exhaustive. You are encouraged to try your own combinations.

SPICES

Chili powder

Cinnamon, ground, and stick

Coriander seeds

Cumin

Fennel seeds

Garlic, whole cloves and powdered

Ginger, fresh, ground, and pickled

Peppercorns, whole, and a good grinder

Red chiles, crushed, whole

Salt: kosher, Maldon

Sesame seeds, black and white

Wasabi powder or paste

FRESH HERBS & PRODUCE

Citrus: grapefruit, lemon, lime, orange, key lime

Herbs: basil, cilantro, dill, mint, flat leaf parsley, thyme

Onions: green, red, white, and yellow

PANTRY

Breadcrumbs, preferably panko if you don't make your own

Capers and olives

Flour, all purpose

Nuts: almonds, pecans, pistachios, walnuts

Sugar: brown, agave honey, sweet sorghum

BUTTER, OILS, VINEGARS & SAUCES

Butter, salted and unsalted

Mayonnaise, light

Miso

Mustard, country-style, Dijon, and dry

Oil: canola, extra virgin olive oil, peanut, sunflower

Ponzu sauce

Soy sauce, low-sodium

Vinegar: apple cider, balsamic, champagne, fig, pear, raspberry, rice wine, white balsamic (you can't have too much vinegar!)

Wine, dry white

Once you get used to a particular flavor profile, switch it up! It's easy to get in a cooking rut. (True story of which I am not proud: In the early 90s, I ate tuna salad with pickled jalapeño on a sesame bagel for lunch every day for a year.)

> Safety equals comfort. Get out of your comfort zone. Play with your food.

Now that you have a go-to pantry list to work from, let's check out the utensils and equipment that will help you become a successful salmon cook.

POTS, PANS AND EVERYDAY KITCHEN TOOLS AND GADGETS

News flash! You do not need expensive or fancy cooking tools or a Food Network–style kitchen to make great-tasting salmon. Whether you cook with gas, electric, or induction heat doesn't matter. Whether you live in a walk-up apartment or a three-story Tudor doesn't matter. Just a few handy kitchen tools and gadgets will help you become a great seafood cook.

To make things fun—I mean, we're talking pots and pans here!—I put together two lists: my fantasy cooking tools list, and my everyday cooking tools list. Let's see how they compare.

My Fantasy Kitchen Tools List

- An eight-burner gas stove with double oven, or an induction stovetop that boils water in 90 seconds.

- Copper pots and pans, or Le Creuset cast-iron cookware, in Caribbean or Flame, please.

- An entire collection of Shun knives or a state-of-the-art Wusthof knife set.

- A mac-daddy stand-up mixer, a personal-size food processor, a Vitamix blender, and a gourmet whip to make frothy foams and creams.

- An assistant—to do my prep and dishes. (Hey, it's *my* fantasy!)

Is your kitchen stocked with my fantasy list? Shoot me an email. I'll be right over. The salmon is on me.

Now that we've established what I don't work with, let's look at what works on a daily basis.

My Everyday Cooking Tools List

- A kitchen timer.

- One 10-inch and one 12-inch stovetop-to-oven skillet, and/or cast-iron skillets, same sizes

- A fish spatula

- Three knives: one nine-inch fillet knife, one ten-inch chef's knife, and a six-inch serrated utility knife

- A knife sharpener

- A set of mixing bowls: small, medium, and large

- Mortar and pestle (or a coffee grinder if you prefer) to grind nuts, seeds, and herbs

- Several baking sheets

- Parchment paper

- A rack that will fit on your baking sheet

- A balloon whisk

- A splatter screen large enough to cover said skillets

Notice how reasonable my everyday list is compared to the dream list? You may already have most of these tools on hand. If you decide to buy new kitchen tools, here are a few handy buying tips:

BUYING TIPS

AIM FOR QUALITY, NOT QUANTITY.

BUY ONE PIECE OF EQUIPMENT AT A TIME, OR WHATEVER YOUR BUDGET ALLOWS.

BUY A SKILLET FIRST. FOR INSTANCE, CAST IRON IS INEXPENSIVE AND AN EXCELLENT PIECE OF EQUIPMENT FOR SEARING SALMON.

If your budget, or the size of your kitchen, doesn't allow for more than one skillet, or if you already own several skillets and none of them is stovetop-to-oven quality, then here's what you do when the recipe states, "Place the skillet in the oven to finish cooking." Using your fish spatula, or a long flat spatula, transfer the fish from the skillet to a baking sheet or shallow oven-safe baking dish to finish cooking the recipe as directed.

Now that you have the shopping chops to know how to buy sustainable salmon, you know how to stock your pantry, and you're cool with what tools to use, you're ready to move on to Chapter 6, Cooking Salmon.

6
COOKING SALMON

Let's face it. One of the reasons salmon is such a popular seafood species is its exceptional nutritional value. Salmon is high in protein, vitamins, minerals, omega-3 fatty acids, and low in fat. It should be no surprise salmon is one of the top eaten seafood species in the world, with triple the production since the 1980s, according to WWF.

But the other reason salmon is so popular? It tastes great! You'll find that you have more time with your family and friends to do the things you love to do. And *that* is always a good thing!

> **The beauty of cooking salmon is simple: less is better.**

With low heat and short cook times, the flesh stays soft, silky, and tender. If you cook salmon too long, the fish's delicate flesh turns tough, chewy, and chalky. One of the most common errors when cooking salmon is overcooking. A kitchen timer will solve that problem. It is your best kitchen gadget friend *and* one of the most essential tools for cooking salmon (or any fresh fish), especially if cooking salmon is new to you. Practice using the timer before you cook anything. Set your timer (the one on your phone will work) for two, three, and four minutes. Go about your business. Notice how quickly time passes? Well, this short amount of time is *critical* when cooking salmon.

Most of the recipes in this book are easy to prepare and quick. Sounds simple enough, right? Not so fast. Let's look at how a few everyday life situations might get in the way of your success for cooking and eating more salmon.

SCENARIO #1

My Grilled Salmon Salad with Beets, Blue Cheese, and Pears recipe is on your weekly meal planner. On your way home from work Wednesday evening you buy a pound of fresh salmon, or four ounces per person. You get home. It's 7:15. You're tired. You put the salmon in the refrigerator. You walk the dog. On your walk, Rex, your lab-shepherd mix, rolls in something unpleasant and needs a bath.

Now it is 8:00 p.m. The kids ate leftovers and your partner is back on the computer working or surfing Facebook. You eat a bowl of cottage cheese and an apple. The salmon goes untouched, wrapped in its store package in the back of the refrigerator.

The next evening you have dinner plans with friends, and Friday is pizza night. Saturday morning, the "fresh" salmon is still in the refrigerator.

If this scenario resembles your life, then please, freeze the salmon for another day as soon as you realize you won't be making it for dinner within one day of buying it.

SCENARIO #2

You want to shed a few pounds and eat lighter meals. You're inspired by this book, and you want to incorporate more salmon into your diet. You buy a piece of salmon at the market and are excited about cooking the Salmon with Pesto and Herbed Goat Cheese Crumbles recipe. You decide to do thirty minutes of yoga before you eat and while in Warrior II Pose, you envision those tiny omega-3 particles coursing through your bloodstream, making you healthier, and more fit after you eat your easy-to-prepare salmon dinner.

You finish yoga and get out your ten-inch skillet. Your phone chirps. It's your best friend telling you to get dressed. There is a wine-tasting with free hors d'oeuvres and beautiful people at your favorite club.

Once again, the salmon goes untouched in its package in the back of the refrigerator.

When this happens, please plan to cook the salmon the next day! For instance, you might have cheeseburgers planned for the neighbors the next evening. In that case follow my recipe for Slow Roasted Salmon, cover and refrigerate it, and then make the Salmon Salad recipe the following day.

You see, there are countless scenarios that will get in the way of you eating salmon, just as there are reasons you don't clean out your email inbox or water the houseplants every Tuesday morning. Life is busy. But don't worry. Once you try these recipes, you will know how much time you need, what ingredients to have on hand, and how delicious and easy these salmon recipes are to make.

Before we dive into the recipes, however, we need to remember one simple rule: cook salmon *eight to ten minutes per inch*, measuring at its thickest point in the center. Of course, not all salmon is one inch thick, so for the majority of the recipes in this book, you will be cooking for less than ten minutes. This fast cooking time is why some find cooking salmon daunting. However, when you practice with a timer, you will become a salmon-cooking expert before you know it.

The recipes in this book are cooked to medium rare to medium temperature, which means the salmon will be warm, but raw in the center, 120 to 125 degrees. If you like your salmon well done, cook *only* one or two minutes longer than the recipe calls for. Remember, salmon will continue to cook a little after you remove it from the heat.

Also note, as salmon cooks, a white substance known as albumin will appear between the flakes of the flesh. This protein resembles cooked egg white and is perfectly edible. The longer you cook salmon, the more albumin you will see. Unless you eat raw salmon, you can expect to see a little albumin on your cooked salmon. You can scrape the albumin off the fish before serving if you prefer.

FISH TIP

COOK SALMON EIGHT TO TEN MINUTES PER INCH OF THICKNESS.

THREE COOKING METHODS

The recipes in Chapter 7 are grouped by cooking method: In The Oven, On The Stove, and On The Grill. All three deliver a rich, satisfying flavor.

In The Oven

One of my favorite ways to prepare salmon is the easiest method—roasted in the oven. Brushed with a little olive oil, air kissed with kosher salt, and dusted with a few cranks of a black pepper mill, the buttery rich flavor of the salmon shines through with roasting. Add a fresh salad and a vegetable for a quick, nutritious everyday meal. If you buy a thick (more than one inch) salmon steak or fillet (usually Alaska king salmon), I suggest you cook the salmon in a skillet on the stovetop for two minutes, turn, and finish roasting it in a 325-degree oven for ten minutes (for medium-rare).

On The Stove

My second favorite method to cook salmon is stovetop-to-oven, similar to roasting, but with one additional step—you must sear the salmon on one side in a skillet on the stovetop before you finish it in a hot oven. You will use the stovetop-to-oven technique when you have thick, meaty cuts of salmon, usually one to two-inches thick.

On The Grill

Whether you grill indoors or outdoors, the technique is similar. Preheat the Foreman griddle or outdoor grill to medium-high heat for several minutes or until you feel the heat rising from the grill when you place your open palm an inch or so above the surface. Turn the heat to medium or medium-low, depending on your equipment. Prepare the surface of the grill or griddle with canola oil and place the salmon top down, or if the skin is on, skin-side down, on the heated surface. Set the timer for two minutes and watch closely as the flesh begins to cook. Flip to the other side and cook two to three minutes longer for medium. You may need to adjust the cook time depending on the thickness of the fish and your equipment. Lower the heat if the fish is browning. Remember, less is better.

COOK'S NOTES

Follow these best practices every time you begin a recipe to make cooking salmon less of an adventure and more of an assured success:

 Read the entire recipe all the way through before you put the first pot on the stove or turn on the oven.

 Prepare your *mise en place*, the fancy French term that literally means "putting in place." For you, this means, "Get organized before you set the oven temperature or turn on the stovetop. Gather the pots, pans, utensils, and all ingredients for the recipe, and set up your work space." Whether that space is your kitchen counter, an island in the middle of the kitchen, or a small chopping block near the toaster oven in your walk-up apartment kitchen, you need to be organized.

 Before you begin to cook, set the table, pour beverages, light the candles, and make sure whoever is eating is within earshot. Salmon cooks fast, and there is nothing worse than making a great meal only to serve it cold because the kids are in their room with the headphones on or your significant other is walking the dog.

 Chop any vegetables or fruit ahead (as early as the day before) to save time. For instance, in the recipe Salmon with Spicy Glazed Peach Salsa, just before you're ready to cook the salmon, combine the salsa ingredients in a bowl and then add the fresh herbs, oil, salt, and pepper.

 Final tip: Clean as you go. You can thank me later.

Let's cook some salmon!

7

EVERYDAY SALMON RECIPES

IN THE OVEN

SLOW ROASTED SALMON SALAD THREE WAYS **60** • HONEY MUSTARD SALMON WITH VERY BERRY VINAIGRETTE **64** • SALMON FLATBREAD WITH MANDARIN ORANGE AND FENNEL **67** • SALMON WITH ROASTED APPLES AND WALNUTS **69** • CUMIN-DUSTED SALMON BOWL WITH PEANUT-THAI SLAW **72** • SLOW ROASTED SALMON WITH BLUEBERRY PAN SAUCE **76** • SALMON IN PARCHMENT **80**

SLOW ROASTED SALMON SALAD
THREE WAYS

SERVES 4

This cold salmon salad is easy to prepare and versatile. Once the salmon is roasted, cooled, and added to the fresh ingredients in the recipe, plop a scoop on a flakey, buttery croissant and add Bibb lettuce for a decadent brunch. Or press it on sourdough and Swiss cheese for a hot melt. Add a side of seasonal fresh fruit for a balanced meal. Or scoop a healthy spoonful on top of mixed greens for a quick, light delicious midweek meal.

> **COOK'S NOTE** | Make salmon salad ahead up to one day to save time. If using canned or pouch salmon, begin recipe at step 5.

1 pound salmon, cut into four equal portions, 4 frozen portions, or 2 cups flaked salmon from a can or pouch

1 tablespoon olive oil

1/2 teaspoon kosher salt

Dash cracked black pepper

1/2 cup red grapes, halved

1/2 cup toasted walnuts, chopped

1 medium celery stalk, sliced thin on the bias, about 1/8-inch thick (about 1/4 cup)

1/4 cup light mayonnaise, for a sweeter-tasting salad, or plain Greek yogurt for a tangy flavor, plus more if desired

2 tablespoons chopped flat leaf parsley

4 teaspoons dried tarragon

2 teaspoons minced shallot

Zest from 1/2 lemon

1 teaspoon lemon juice

1. Arrange a rack in the center of the oven, and preheat oven to 275 degrees.

2. Line a baking sheet with parchment paper or spray with cooking oil.

3. Rub the salmon on all sides with olive oil and season with kosher salt and black pepper.

4. Place the salmon on the baking sheet and place in the oven. Roast for 30 minutes.

5. While the salmon roasts, add the grapes, walnuts, and celery to a large mixing bowl.

6. When the salmon has finished roasting, remove from the oven and let it rest and cool about 15 minutes or until the salmon is cool to the touch.

7. Flake the salmon portions with a fork and add to the fresh ingredients in the large bowl.

8. Add the mayonnaise, parsley, tarragon, shallot, lemon zest, and lemon juice, and stir.

9. Serve immediately or cover and refrigerate for up to one day.

HONEY MUSTARD SALMON
WITH VERY BERRY VINAIGRETTE

SERVES 6-8

Slow roasting a whole salmon fillet is one of the easiest ways to prepare salmon. In this recipe, the entire fillet goes in the oven on a baking sheet. And you don't check on it until you are ready to add the mustard glaze five minutes before the salmon is done cooking. The vinaigrette adds a much-needed sweetness to complement the tangy mustard, but drizzle judiciously over the salmon, as too much will overpower the fish. Serve the vinaigrette on the side in a small dish if desired. The vinaigrette also doubles as a salad dressing, so if you want more for your greens, just double the ingredients.

Very Berry Vinaigrette

- 1/4 cup fresh raspberries
- 1 teaspoon strawberry jam
- 1 teaspoon blackberry jam
- 1/4 teaspoon agave or honey
- 1 tablespoon balsamic vinegar

Very Berry Vinaigrette (cont.)

Dash kosher salt

Dash black pepper

Honey Mustard Salmon

3 tablespoons olive oil, plus more if desired

1 tablespoon country mustard

1 tablespoon Dijon mustard

1 garlic clove, minced

1/2 teaspoon chopped fresh rosemary

1 tablespoon olive oil

Splash of white wine

Dash dried thyme

1 side of salmon, 1-1/2 to 2 pounds, skin on

2 tablespoons canola oil

Kosher salt

Black pepper

To make the vinaigrette:

1. Add raspberries, strawberry jam, and blackberry jam to a medium bowl. Muddle the fruit with the jam.

2. Add the honey, balsamic, salt, and pepper to the bowl. Stir.

3. Whisk in the olive oil, slowly, to emulsify the vinaigrette. Vinaigrette will be smooth with small bits of fruit. Add more oil, if desired. Set aside.

To make the salmon:

1. Arrange a rack in the center of the oven. Preheat the oven to 300 degrees.

2. Line a baking sheet with parchment paper. The baking sheet should be large enough to hold the entire side of salmon.

3. Add the country mustard, Dijon mustard, garlic, rosemary, olive oil, wine, and thyme to a small bowl. Stir. Taste and season with salt and black pepper.

4. Arrange a salmon fillet on the lined baking sheet. Pat the salmon dry with paper towels.

5. Rub the canola oil over the top of the fish. Sprinkle with salt and pepper.

6. Place the salmon in the oven and roast 20 minutes. Brush the mustard mix over the top of the entire salmon and bake for 5 minutes longer.

7. Using two long spatulas, transfer the fish to a large platter. Spoon small amounts of Very Berry Vinaigrette over the top, or serve in a bowl on the side. Serve immediately.

SALMON FLATBREAD
WITH MANDARIN ORANGE AND FENNEL

SERVES 4

Slivers of fennel-flavored salmon, mandarin oranges, tangy mustard, and Swiss cheese make this easy-to-prepare flatbread a crowd-pleaser. I use store-bought crust to save time, but feel free to make your own! Serve with mixed greens for a balanced meal.

1 shallot, cut into slivers

1 tablespoon butter

1 store-bought crust

2 tablespoons Dijon mustard

2 tablespoons olive oil

1 cup low-fat grated Swiss cheese

1 large tomato, sliced and patted dry

1 (10.5-ounce) can Mandarin oranges, drained

1 teaspoon fennel seeds, toasted and crushed

Kosher salt

Black pepper

Olive oil

8 ounces salmon, skin removed, cut into 1/2-inch strips

1. Preheat the oven to 450 degrees.
2. Melt butter in a small skillet over medium heat.
3. Add the shallots and cook about 2 minutes, careful not to brown. Remove from heat. Let shallots sit in the warm skillet while you prepare the flatbread.
4. Mix the mustard, olive oil, and a teaspoon of water in a small bowl. Spread on the crust.
5. Distribute the cheese over the top.
6. Arrange tomato slices and mandarin orange over the cheese.
7. Bake in a 450-degree oven for 5 minutes.
8. While the flatbread bakes, sprinkle oil, fennel, salt, and pepper over salmon in a medium bowl. Stir to coat.
9. Remove the flatbread, add the salmon and shallots, and return to the oven to cook and additional 5 minutes.
10. Remove from oven. Let rest for 5 minutes. Slice and serve.

SALMON
WITH ROASTED APPLES AND WALNUTS

SERVES 4

Got apples? This quick recipe will have you rethinking baked apples as just a dessert item. Plus, the zing from the yogurt, the bite from the horseradish, and the fresh cool mint complement the sweet apples and salmon. Serve with a fresh spinach salad, steamed broccoli, or Caesar salad for a balanced meal.

> **COOK'S NOTE** | Make apples up to two days and walnuts up to one week to save time. Use a crisp, tart apple like Honeycrisp, Granny Smith, or Fuji, or use Asian pear, which is similar to an apple, if it is available in your market.

2 to 3 apples, cored, sliced or diced

Juice of 1/2 lemon; reserve skin for zest (if desired)

2 tablespoons brown sugar

1 teaspoon cinnamon

Dash nutmeg

1 cup walnut halves and pieces

Canola oil

Kosher salt

Dash black pepper

4 (4-ounce) salmon portions, skin removed

1/3 cup low-fat plain Greek yogurt

1/2 to 3/4 teaspoon fresh ground horseradish, more or less for desired bite

Lemon zest, if desired

1 tablespoon chopped fresh mint

1. Preheat oven to 400 degrees.

2. Add apples to a medium bowl. Squeeze lemon juice over the apples and stir.

3. Add brown sugar, cinnamon, and nutmeg. Stir to coat apples.

4. Line a baking sheet with parchment paper and spread the apples on the lined baking sheet. Do not crowd the apples.

5. Place the apples in a 400-degree oven for 15 to 20 minutes or until desired doneness. This is subjective. You may like your apples soft and creamy; if so, bake a little longer. Remove from oven.

6. Reduce the oven temperature to 350 degrees.

7. Spread walnuts on a parchment-lined baking sheet in an even layer and bake for 8 minutes.

8. While walnuts bake, rinse the salmon under cold water and pat dry.

9. Rub canola oil over the salmon and sprinkle salt and black pepper over the salmon.

10. When the walnuts are toasted, remove the nuts from baking sheet to a bowl to cool. Reserve the parchment paper for the salmon.

11. Place salmon portions on the warm parchment-lined baking sheet. Place in the oven and roast for 10 minutes per inch of thickness. Adjust time as needed for the size of fish you are using.

12. While the salmon roasts, add horseradish and lemon zest to yogurt in a small bowl. Stir.

13. Remove the salmon from the oven and arrange the cooked salmon on a plate or platter for family-style serving.

14. Top roasted salmon with apples. Plop a small amount of yogurt on top of the apples or on the side. Sprinkle walnuts and fresh mint on salmon.

15. Serve immediately with couscous and a fresh green salad or side of steamed green beans.

CUMIN-DUSTED SALMON BOWL WITH PEANUT-THAI SLAW

SERVES 4

The Cumin-Dusted Salmon Bowl was, without a doubt, one of the easiest recipes to develop for *Salmon*. But what makes this recipe so exciting for me is that it is simple enough for even my husband (the one who doesn't cook in my family) to make. If you like crunchy, sweet, spicy food that satisfies, then you'll love this recipe.

> **COOK'S NOTE**
>
> To save time, make the Peanut Butter Vinaigrette up to one week ahead, and the slaw up to two days ahead. Store in separate covered containers in the refrigerator.

Peanut Chili Vinaigrette
yield: 3/4 cup

- 2 tablespoons creamy peanut butter
- 2 tablespoons rice vinegar
- 2 tablespoons ponzu (citrus-flavored soy sauce)
- 1 tablespoon agave
- 1/4 teaspoon crushed red pepper flakes
- Dash kosher salt
- Black pepper
- 6 tablespoons olive oil

Thai Slaw

- 3 cups shredded Napa cabbage, or 1/2 large head (substitute iceberg)
- 1 medium carrot, cleaned and shredded
- 1 medium celery stalk, sliced thin on the bias, about 1/8-inch thick
- 1/2 red bell pepper, sliced into slivers and cut in thirds

Thai Slaw (cont.)	1 teaspoon shallot, sliced on lowest setting on mandolin, or diced
	3 tablespoons chopped flat leaf parsley

1 cup uncooked jasmine rice

4 (4-ounce) salmon portions

Olive oil

Kosher salt and freshly ground black pepper

1 teaspoon cumin

1/2 teaspoon garlic powder

1/2 teaspoon red pepper flakes

1 avocado sliced or cut into cubes, if desired

1. Preheat oven to 325 degrees.

2. Place peanut butter, rice vinegar, ponzu, agave, red pepper flakes, salt, and pepper in a small bowl. Whisk until mixture is creamy, about 1 minute. Adding 2 tablespoons of olive oil at a time, whisk until oil is emulsified. Reserve vinaigrette at room temperature until you are ready to serve.

3. In a medium bowl, add cabbage, carrot, celery, bell pepper, shallot, and parsley. Mix.

4. Prepare rice according to package directions.

5. While rice cooks, line a baking sheet with parchment paper. Spray parchment with cooking spray. Place salmon portions on the lined baking sheet. Rub a small amount of olive oil into the flesh of the fish. Sprinkle salt and black pepper over each portion like an air kiss. Sprinkle cumin, garlic powder, and red pepper flakes over each portion evenly.

6. Place baking sheet in preheated oven and set your timer for 10 minutes. Test for doneness by placing a thermostat in the thickest part of the fish for several seconds, then place the thermostat on the inside of your wrist. If the thermostat is not warm, bake a few more minutes or until desired doneness using the 10 minutes per inch cooking rule. Remove the salmon from the oven and tent with foil while you plate the salad and rice.

7. Scoop a half cup of rice into each bowl. Add an equal amount of slaw. Drizzle the Peanut Butter Vinaigrette over the slaw mix. Place the salmon in the bowl. Add avocado. Serve immediately.

SLOW ROASTED SALMON
WITH BLUEBERRY PAN SAUCE

SERVES 6

Alaska salmon fishermen Jason & Mary Beth McKinley live in Central Kentucky, yet each summer they travel to the pristine icy waters of Bristol Bay, Alaska to fish for sockeye salmon. These entrepreneurs are a shining example of what it takes to support sustainable fisheries. Like them, when you work hard, you need a no-fuss meal with a boatload of flavor. This easy-to-prepare recipe was made with Jason & Mary Beth in mind. Thanks CaughtWildSalmon!

> **COOK'S NOTE** | Remove salmon from the refrigerator 30 minutes to bring to room temperature. Pat dry. Remove pin bones with tweezers if needed. Season the salmon flesh with salt, pepper, half of the dried thyme, and the fresh parsley.

1 whole two-pound Alaska sockeye salmon fillet, skin on, bones out

1/4 teaspoons dried thyme, divided in half

Dash sea salt

Dash black pepper

1 teaspoon parsley, chopped

1 tablespoon canola oil, plus more to grease foil lined baking sheet

6 ounces fresh organic blueberries

1 tablespoon sugar

1 teaspoon balsamic vinegar

1 teaspoon lemon juice, plus zest for garnish

Shallot, slivers

1. Preheat the oven to 275 degrees.

2. Line a large baking sheet with foil and use either a cooking spray to lightly coat the foil or brush the foil with oil.

3. Arrange the salmon on the foil lined baking sheet, skin side down and place the tray in the preheated oven. Roast for 20 to 25 minutes, depending on the salmon thickness.

4. While the salmon is roasting, make the Chile Oil and Blueberry Pan Sauce.

5. To make the Chile Oil, pour the olive oil in a small dish. Add the red pepper flakes, salt, pepper, and powdered ginger. Stir.

6. To make the Blueberry Pan Sauce, add the blueberries, sugar, balsamic vinegar and the other 1/8 teaspoon dried thyme in a small saucepan on medium heat. Bring to a slow boil.

7. Listen for a sound like a snap or a pop to indicate the sugar is melting. Begin to mash and stir the berries with a wooden spoon.

8. Bring the berries to a boil, reduce the heat to medium low, stirring occasionally, breaking up the berries. Cook for 5 minutes. Remove the pan from the heat. Add a pinch of salt and the lemon juice. Stir.

9. Remove the salmon from the oven and test for doneness. If the thickest part of the salmon flakes easily, the salmon is done.

10. Transfer the salmon to a large serving platter. Arrange the sauce on and around fish, or on the side if you prefer. Add the fresh shallot slivers and zest the lemon over the top. Serve the Chile Oil on the side or spoon it over fish as you serve.

11. To save time, make the Blueberry Pan Sauce ahead up to several days. Cover and refrigerate. Warm the sauce before serving.

SALMON
IN PARCHMENT

SERVES 4

There is something about baking fresh Alaska salmon and bright fresh vegetables in parchment that not only works as a quick midweek meal, it shines as an elegant, impressive dinner. When salmon is easy, delicious, good for you, and the oceans.

> **COOK'S NOTE** | To save time, the butter beans and sauce can be made ahead up to one day. Cover and refrigerate until ready to cook.

1 pound butter beans, in shell

2 tablespoon white miso

2 tablespoons honey

2 tablespoons Ponzu sauce

1 teaspoon orange juice

½ teaspoon rice vinegar

¼ teaspoon red pepper flakes

Dash ginger powder

Dash salt

Dash black pepper

1 medium zucchini

1 medium yellow squash

1 small shallot

4 six-ounce Alaska sockeye salmon portions, skinless, boneless

2 small oranges

4 fresh thyme sprigs (sub basil if desired)

1. Preheat the oven to 400 degrees.

2. Remove salmon from refrigerator. Pat dry with paper towels.

3. Fold parchment paper in half and cut the open side to resembled half a heart. Open the paper. It will look like a heart. Using a basting brush, apply olive oil on centers of both sides of parchment using a light stroke. Or spray lightly with baking spray.

4. Bring water to boil in a medium saucepan.

5. Shell the butter beans. Add the beans to the boiling water. Reduce the heat to medium low and simmer 4 to 5 minutes. Strain the beans from the water and plunge them into an ice bath for 4 minutes. Strain again to paper towels to dry.

6. Whisk the miso, honey, ponzu, orange juice, rice vinegar, pepper flakes, ginger, salt and pepper in a small bowl.

7. Cut the zucchini and yellow squash into ½ inch slices.

8. Cut the shallot into paper-thin slices.

9. Cut the oranges (or lemons if desired) into four equal slices each about ½ inch thick.

10. Arrange the cut parchment papers on a large baking sheet. Use two baking sheets if needed.

11. Arrange the zucchini, yellow squash and shallots on one side of the parchment near the fold making a bed for the salmon. Spoon a little of the sauce over the vegetables.

12. Place the salmon on top of the vegetable bed.

13. Divide the butter beans between the four salmon parchments and scatter around the salmon.

14. Lay two orange slices on the tops of the salmon.

15. Place one thyme sprig on each of the orange slices.

16. Spoon the remaining sauce over the tops of the salmon dividing equally.

17. Fold the top parchment paper over the salmon. Start at top of the heart and begin to fold the parchment closed, overlapping and sealing the folds as you move around the outer, open edge.

18. Twist the bottom closed.

19. Place the tray of parchment-wrapped salmon in the preheated oven and roast for ten minutes.

20. Remove the salmon in parchment to serving plates. Cut or tear the parchment at one end. Be careful as steam will escape. Cut up the center of the parchment, turning and folding the parchment away from the center. Serve immediately.

ON THE STOVE

FARMERS MARKET SALMON SALAD 86 • SALMON WITH SPICY PEACH SALSA 90 • SUMMER SALMON CHOWDER 93 • POACHED SALMON WITH CHEESE GRITS AND EGGS 96 • SPICY SALMON RICE BOWL 99 • SALMON WITH ORANGE-BOURBON GLAZE 101 • SIMPLE STEAMED SALMON 104 • MEDITERRANEAN SALMON WITH CHICKPEA MASH 106 • SALMON CORN CHOWDER 109 • SALMON BURGER WITH CRANBERRY YOGURT 112 • PAN-GRILLED SALMON WITH CILANTRO-WALNUT PESTO 116

FARMERS MARKET
SALMON SALAD

SERVES 4

This healthy bowlful-of-sunshine salad is the quintessential summertime meal. Use a few basic kitchen staples, like eggs and olives, and add vegetables from the farmers market (or your garden) to round out the creamy, crunchy, briny earthiness of this satisfying salad. Drizzle champagne vinegar and olive oil over the top for a quick pop of flavor.

2 eggs

8 baby white or fingerling potatoes

1 pound green beans

1 head red leaf or Bibb lettuce

2 tomatoes

4 (4-ounce) salmon portions, skin removed

1/4 cup kalamata olives, pitted

Several sprigs of fresh basil, parsley, or cilantro, chopped (or whatever fresh herb is in your garden)

Dash kosher salt

Dash black pepper

1. Place the eggs in a medium saucepan, cover with cold water an inch over the eggs, and bring to a rapid boil over medium-high heat. Reduce to a simmer and cook 4 to 5 minutes for a firm but creamy yolk. Drain the pan and fill with cold water. Let the eggs sit in cold water about 5 minutes to stop the cooking process. Peel and quarter.

2. Boil the potatoes in a medium pot of water until tender, depending on the size of your potatoes, about 10 minutes. Drain.

3. While the potatoes cook, steam the green beans for 4 to 5 minutes and then plunge them into a bowl of ice water. Let them chill for several minutes. Remove the beans from the ice bath and dry them on paper towels.

4. Wash lettuce and spin dry, or towel dry if you don't have a spinner.

5. Wash and chop tomatoes.

6. Pat the salmon dry with paper towels. Sprinkle both sides of the salmon with kosher salt and black pepper.

7. Heat a skillet over medium heat. Place the salmon top-side down and cook about 2 minutes. Resist the urge to move the fish. Reduce heat to medium low if fish is browning. Turn and continue to cook another 3 to 4 minutes for medium, depending on the thickness of the salmon.

8. While the salmon cooks, arrange the lettuce either in individual bowls or on a large platter for family-style dining. Arrange tomatoes, green beans, olives, and eggs over lettuce, reserving space for the salmon.

9. Place salmon on lettuce bed. Sprinkle fresh herbs over the entire salad. Splash vinegar and oil or dressing of your choice over the top. Serve immediately.

SALMON
WITH SPICY PEACH SALSA

SERVES 4

This recipe is quick and easy. Once the salmon is cooked, simply plop a spoonful of Spicy Peach Salsa on top and serve. The mix of sweet, tender peaches and crunchy peppers with a pop of heat complement the sweet, flaky salmon. Paired with salad greens and a steamed vegetable, this recipe is a balanced midweek meal or a weekend crowd-pleaser.

> **COOK'S NOTE** | Thaw frozen salmon twenty-four hours in the refrigerator before you cook it. Cover and refrigerate unused portions of the salsa and use within two days.

Spicy Peach Salsa

- 4 tablespoons honey
- 1 tablespoon water
- 1 tablespoon lemon juice
- 1 teaspoon sriracha
- 1 teaspoon Dijon mustard

Spicy Peach Salsa (cont.)

	4 medium peaches, peeled and chopped (about 2 cups)
	2 tablespoons chopped jalapeño peppers, seeds and rib removed
	2 tablespoons chopped red bell peppers
	2 tablespoons chopped yellow peppers
	2 tablespoons chopped orange bell peppers
	1 teaspoon diced shallots
	3 teaspoons sugar
	1/2 teaspoon lemon juice
	1/4 cup chopped fresh cilantro
	4 (4- to 6-ounce) salmon portions, skin removed
	1 tablespoon canola oil
	Kosher salt
	Black pepper

To make the salsa:

1. Add honey, water, lemon juice, hot sauce, and Dijon mustard to a medium saucepan and bring to a simmer over medium heat. Cook about 10 minutes, stirring occasionally.

The glaze will reduce and become slightly sticky. Remove from heat.

2. Add chopped peaches, jalapeño, red, yellow, and orange peppers, and shallots to the warm glaze. Stir to coat.

3. Transfer the peach salsa to a medium bowl. Add cilantro and stir. Set aside.

To make the salmon:

1. Pat salmon dry. Sprinkle the salmon portions on both sides with kosher salt and black pepper. Use a light touch, like an air kiss.

2. Get out the kitchen timer—this next step happens fast. Heat a skillet over medium-high heat for 3 to 4 minutes.

3. Add a tablespoon of canola oil and swirl in the pan.

4. Place the salmon portions in the skillet flesh-side down. Immediately reduce the heat to medium low and set the timer for 2 minutes.

5. After 2 minutes, turn and cook another 2 minutes on the other side for medium rare. Adjust cook time for thicker portions, using 10 minutes per inch of thickness as a guide.

6. Remove the salmon from heat at the desired temperature.

7. Top with salsa and serve immediately.

SUMMER
SALMON CHOWDER

SERVES 6-8

Soup during summer? You bet. Bring fresh garden vegetables and peak seasonal salmon into the kitchen with this easy-to-prepare chowder. Cream-style corn adds a silky texture to this chunky, delicious soup.

> **COOK'S NOTE** | Refrigerate uneaten chowder for up to two days. Warm on the stovetop on low for best results.

4 tablespoons olive oil

3 medium celery stalks, chopped

3 medium carrots, chopped

1 small Vidalia or Candy onion, chopped

10 small okra, chopped, stems discarded

1 medium red or orange bell pepper, chopped

1 medium jalapeño chopped, half seeds removed

2 cups corn from kernel or frozen

1 (15-ounce) can sweet corn cream style

6 cups low-sodium vegetable or chicken stock

1 teaspoon cumin

2 bay leaves

1 teaspoon kosher salt

Dash black pepper

1 1/2 pounds salmon, skin removed, cut into 1- to 2-ounce pieces

Flat leaf parsley, chopped, if desired for garnish

1. Heat olive oil in a large stock pan over medium heat.
2. Add the celery, carrots, onion, okra, bell pepper, and jalapeño to the pan. Stir to coat the vegetables with oil.
3. Cook the vegetables 4 to 5 minutes or until onion and celery are translucent.
4. Add fresh corn and cream corn, and stir.
5. Add the stock, cumin, bay leaves, salt, and pepper.
6. Cover with a vented lid, reduce heat, and simmer for 20 minutes or until carrots are tender. Stir occasionally.
7. Increase heat to medium and add salmon pieces, stirring as you add. Cook uncovered for 5 minutes or until salmon pieces are cooked.
8. Turn off heat and let chowder sit 5 minutes.

9. Remove bay leaves and discard.

10. Ladle chowder into bowls. Garnish with flat leaf parsley. Serve immediately.

POACHED SALMON
WITH CHEESE GRITS AND EGGS

SERVES 4

Small salmon portions are poached in a wine and water bath, served over warm, creamy cheese and green chile grits, and then topped with a poached egg (or fried, if desired) to round out this breakfast-for-dinner meal.

> **COOK'S NOTE** | Grits will harden as they cool, so either keep them warm in a double boiler or add a few tablespoons of boiling water to the pot and stir before serving. Use either quick-cooking or slow-cooking grits, whichever you prefer or have in your pantry.

Boil an additional 1 cup of water in a teakettle or microwave as a reserve in case you need to add water to the pan for the poached salmon or eggs.

Grits for 4

1 (4-ounce) can diced green chiles

1/2 cup shredded Monterey Jack cheese

Dry white wine

4 (4-ounce) salmon portions, skin removed

4 eggs

Kosher salt

Black pepper

Fresh cilantro

1. Prepare grits according to package directions for four servings.

2. When grits are finished cooking, add green chiles and cheese. Stir. Keep warm.

3. Bring 4 cups of water and a splash of white wine to a boil in a wide, deep skillet. Add the salmon, cover with a lid, and return to a boil. How long this takes will depend on how big your pan is. When the water boils, remove the lid and reduce heat to low. Water will barely be simmering. Cook for 4 minutes for medium, or until desired doneness. Remove salmon with a fish spatula or slotted spoon and dry on paper towel. Tent with foil to keep warm.

4. Increase heat to medium so that water is bubbling from the bottom of the pan. Add a little of the reserved boiling water to pan if needed.

5. Crack an egg into a small dish and slide the egg into the hot water. Repeat until all eggs are in the water. Cook 3 to 4 minutes for medium, more or less for desired doneness. Remove the eggs with a slotted spoon and place on a paper towel.

6. Place a spoonful of prepared grits in a bowl or plate. Top with salmon, then the poached eggs. Sprinkle salt and pepper over the top.

7. Garnish with fresh cilantro and serve immediately.

SPICY SALMON RICE BOWL

SERVES 6-8

When I crave spicy, sweet, and warm food, Spicy Salmon Rice Bowl is my go-to recipe. Made with a few basic ingredients always in my pantry, I never worry about dashing to the store for that "special" ingredient. Warning: You'll be eating in less than 30 minutes. Ready, set, cook!

1 cup uncooked jasmine rice

1 tablespoon olive oil

1/4 cup chopped red bell pepper

1 small Vidalia or Candy onion, chopped

1 garlic clove, minced

3 cups chopped tomatoes with juice

1 tablespoon chili garlic paste

1 tablespoon light mayonnaise or Greek plain yogurt, if desired

4 (4- to 6-ounce) salmon portions

A handful of fresh cilantro leaves, chopped, if desired

1. Prepare rice according to package directions.

2. While rice is cooking, heat a large skillet over medium heat.

3. Add olive oil, swirling to coat the bottom of the skillet, and add the onions and peppers. Cook, stirring occasionally, about 5 minutes or until onions begin to soften and turn translucent. Reduce heat to avoid browning the onions.

4. Add garlic; stir and cook 1 minute or less.

5. Add tomatoes and juice, chili paste, and mayonnaise, and stir.

6. Add salmon portions. Nestle the salmon in the sauce and spoon a little over the tops. Cover, reduce heat to medium-low, and cook 10 to 15 minutes depending on the thickness of the portions.

7. Remove the lid at desired doneness and sprinkle the fresh cilantro over the fish, spooning the sauce over the top of the fish again. Remove from heat.

8. Fluff rice and scoop a healthy spoonful into a bowl. Top with a salmon portion and spoon sauce over the top. Serve immediately.

SALMON
WITH ORANGE-BOURBON GLAZE

SERVES 4

As any Kentuckian will tell you, the Bluegrass State is defined by horses, hoops, and bourbon, and not necessarily in that order. Naturally, I am proud to include a bourbon-inspired salmon recipe. Bourbon flavors range from mild to bold, from smooth to smoky, and impart vanilla, caramel, fruity, tobacco and chocolate notes. I recommend a mild bourbon for this recipe.

> **COOK'S NOTE**
>
> You can make this recipe without the bourbon, but you will lose the dusty, smoky flavor that rounds out the sweetness in the Orange Glaze. Sorghum is Kentucky's maple syrup or honey, depending on which part of the Commonwealth you live in. Feel free to use either maple syrup or honey if you can't find sorghum in your market.

2 teaspoons white sesame seeds

2 teaspoons brown sugar

1/4 teaspoon salt

1/4 teaspoon flour or cornstarch

1/2 cup orange juice

2 tablespoons Kentucky sorghum

2 tablespoons vinegar

1 tablespoon bourbon

1/4 teaspoon salt

2 teaspoons cornstarch

Dash red pepper flakes

4 (6-ounce) salmon portions

1 to 2 tablespoons canola oil

Dash kosher salt

Dash black pepper

1. Place sesame seeds, brown sugar, salt, and flour in a small bowl. Stir.

2. Whisk the orange juice, sorghum, vinegar, bourbon, salt, cornstarch, and red pepper in a small saucepan over medium heat. Cook and stir for several minutes to heat throughout and combine flavors. Remove from heat. Keep warm, or reheat and stir before serving.

3. Rinse salmon in cold water and pat dry.

4. Rub canola oil over the salmon. Sprinkle salt and black pepper over the top.

5. Sprinkle one-fourth of the dry sesame and sugar mix over the top of each salmon portion, pressing the mix into the flesh.

6. Heat a 12-inch skillet over medium heat for several minutes.

7. Place the salmon, top-side down in the skillet. Cook 1 to 2 minutes. Turn and cook another 3 to 4 minutes for medium, or until desired doneness.

8. Spoon the warm glaze over the fish. Serve immediately with fresh asparagus in spring, succotash in summer, and mashed potatoes or squash in fall and winter.

SIMPLE STEAMED SALMON

SERVES 4

I love to eat pizza, dark chocolate, and cheese of any kind. But since moderation is key, I know to eat healthy as well. When I indulge and need to get back on track with my diet, I reach for my foldout steamer basket and skin-off salmon. Often overlooked, and one of the easiest ways to cook salmon, steaming keeps the fish tender and flakey without a lot of fuss or ingredients. Add a plate of fresh vegetables, a scoop of jasmine rice, and a dash of soy sauce and lemon juice for a light, day-after-the-party meal.

> **COOK'S NOTE** | Keep a cup of boiling water handy to add to the pan if necessary.

2 ounces dry white wine

4 (4-ounce) salmon portions, skin removed

Dash salt

Dash black pepper

4 fresh fennel fronds or dill sprigs

4 lemon wedges

Soy sauce, if desired

1. Pat salmon dry.

2. Sprinkle the top of the salmon with salt and pepper.

3. Lay one fennel frond or dill sprig over the top of each salmon portion.

4. Add a half-inch of water and the white wine to a wide saucepan.

5. Place a foldout steamer basket in the saucepan. Make sure the basket sits above the liquid. Cover and bring the liquid to a boil over high heat.

6. When the water boils, place the salmon in the basket, cover, and steam for 6 to 8 minutes depending on the thickness. Add boiling water to the pan if necessary, careful not to pour water on the salmon.

7. Remove the salmon from the steamer basket and spritz the top of the salmon with lemon juice. Serve immediately with rice, vegetable, and soy sauce on the side.

MEDITERRANEAN SALMON
WITH CHICKPEA MASH

SERVES 4

I traveled to Israel in the early 1990s and have been fascinated with flavors of the Mediterranean diet since. While there, I witnessed my first blood red sunrise. We had traveled through the Negev Desert and stopped for breakfast in a communal dining hall. Hungry for sustenance, I found not a typical American breakfast of pancakes, bacon, eggs, and cold cereal, but rather large bowls of yogurt, hard-boiled eggs, dried fruits, fish in oil, hummus, and olives. When I think of that trip, I am transported back to that simple, delicious time and cook this easy, flavorful recipe.

> **COOK'S NOTE** | If salmon portions are more than 1-inch thick, preheat oven to 325 degrees. You will need to cook the salmon on the stovetop and then finish cooking it in the oven. Otherwise, this is a one-skillet recipe.

1 (15-ounce) can chickpeas

1 tablespoon minced shallot

8 kalamata olives, pitted and chopped, or 2 tablespoons

1/2 lemon, for juice and zest

Olive oil

1 radish, for zest

1 tablespoon fresh mint, chopped, plus sprigs for garnish, if desired

1 to 2 tablespoons plain Greek yogurt, more or less to taste, if desired

4 (4- to 6-ounce) salmon portions, skin removed

Canola oil

Kosher salt

Black pepper

To make the Chickpea Mash:

1. Drain the chickpeas. Pour them into a medium bowl and use a potato masher to smash them a bit. Don't be too aggressive; you want a chunky mash.

2. Add the shallot, olives, lemon juice, and lemon zest to the bowl and stir. Drizzle olive oil and stir to coat. Season with kosher salt and black pepper. Stir. Taste and add more salt and pepper if desired.

3. Zest the radish, red portion only, into the bowl; add the mint and stir again.

4. For a creamier texture and to soften the Chickpea Mash, add a few tablespoons of yogurt and stir, or serve yogurt on the side.

To make the salmon:

1. Pat the salmon dry. Rub the salmon with canola oil and season both sides with salt and pepper.

2. Heat a nonstick skillet over medium heat. Add salmon, top-side down. Cook for 2 minutes. Turn and continue cooking for 2 to 3 minutes longer. If salmon portions are thicker than 1 inch, place in a preheated 325-degree oven for desired doneness.

3. Arrange a spoonful of Chickpea Mash on a plate. Place the salmon on top of the mash. Plop a spoonful of yogurt on the salmon. Garnish with mint. Serve immediately.

SALMON CORN CHOWDER

SERVES 4-6

The fresh, simple flavors of sweet corn and fresh salmon scream summertime. Yet frozen corn and frozen salmon during the cold winter months work equally as well. Salmon Corn Chowder is the perfect, one-pot, midweek meal during the long, sultry days of summer or the short cold days of winter.

2 tablespoons butter

2 tablespoons olive oil

2 medium carrots, diced, ½ cup

2 stalks celery, diced, ½ cup

1 shallot, diced or ¼ cup

2 cups corn, divided

Dash kosher Salt

Dash pepper

¼ teaspoon thyme

3 cups corn stock

3 medium Yukon gold potatoes, diced, or 2 cups

Flat leaf parsley, garnish

1 pound salmon cut in three-quarter inch strips, skin off

Tomato, diced (optional)

1. Heat a large stockpot on medium heat. Add butter and oil. When butter foams, add carrots, celery and shallots, stir and cook about 4 to 5 minutes until onion and celery are translucent.

2. While mire poix is cooking, pulverize one cup of corn and one tablespoons water in food processor until thick and paste-like.

3. Add pureed corn, potatoes, thyme, salt and pepper to pot. Stir and cover with vented lid. Bring to soft boil. Reduce heat to medium low. Cook for ten to eleven minutes. Press down with back of wooden spoon to mash some of the potatoes when they are fork tender.

4. Add remaining cup of corn and salmon. Stir. Cook 3 to 4 minutes or until salmon flesh is opaque and corn warm.

5. Stir in fresh parsley.

6. Ladle into bowls. Serve immediately.

SALMON BURGER
WITH CRANBERRY YOGURT

SERVES 6

What makes this salmon burger so exceptionally delicious is the salmon! Copper River Silver salmon is silky and full of flavor creating a melt-in-your-mouth burger. A few savory flavors complement the sweet, delicate texture of this sought-after salmon species. Appetite required.

1 teaspoon unsalted butter

1 teaspoon olive oil

2 celery stalk hearts, diced or 1/3 cup

1 small shallot, minced or 1 tablespoon

Dash kosher salt

Dash black pepper

1.25-1.50 pound salmon fillet, skin off

½ cup panko bread crumbs

½ cup light mayonnaise

2 tablespoons flat leaf parsley, chopped

1 teaspoon Dijon mustard

1 teaspoon salt

¼ teaspoon black pepper

½ cup Greek plain yogurt

1 tablespoon, plus 1 teaspoon chopped dried cranberries

1 teaspoon chopped cilantro

¼ teaspoon lemon juice

Zest from half a lemon

¼ cup all-purpose flour

1 tablespoon canola oil, plus more if needed

Slider buns

1 cucumber

Baby romaine lettuce

1. Heat a medium skillet on medium heat for several minutes. Add butter and oil. When butter foams, add celery, stir, and cook 2 minutes.

2. Add the minced shallots. Season celery and shallots lightly with salt and pepper. Stir continuously for 1 minute to take the edge off the vegetables. Remove from heat and transfer to a large bowl to cool.

3. Cut two-thirds of the salmon into large chunks. Place the large chunks in a food processor and pulse about ten times. Add to the bowl.

4. Chop the remaining one-third into ½ inch chunks. Add to the bowl.

5. Add the panko, mayonnaise, parsley, mustard, salt and pepper to the bowl. Stir until all ingredients are blended.

6. Form into six patties and place on a parchment lined platter or baking sheet. Cover with plastic wrap and refrigerate for two to three hours and up to one day.

7. While salon burgers chill, add yogurt, dried cranberries, cilantro, lemon juice and zest to a small bowl. Stir. Cover and refrigerate.

8. When you're ready to cook, remove salmon burgers from refrigerator.

9. Add flour, salt and pepper to a shallow dish. Dredge salmon burgers in the flour. Wipe off excess to leave a fine coating.

10. Heat a large skillet on medium heat for several minutes. Reduce heat to medium low and add canola oil. Swirl pan. Oil should shimmer.

11. Place salmon burgers in the skillet. Do not crowd. Work in batches if necessary. Cook for 3 minutes. Flip once and cook 3 additional minutes. Remove from heat.

12. While salmon cooks, split buns and slice cucumbers.

13. Remove the Cranberry Yogurt from the refrigerator.

14. Arrange the buns on a platter. Layer lettuce, cucumbers, then salmon on the bun bottoms. Plop a dollop of yogurt on top of the salmon. Add the bun lid. Serve immediately.

PAN-GRILLED SALMON
WITH CILANTRO-WALNUT PESTO

SERVES 4

Bold, bright, nutty flavors punch up this easy-to-prepare recipe. Pair the salmon with a lemon-scented jasmine rice or quinoa. Add a hearty tossed salad for a quick, balanced, meal.

4 six-ounce salmon fillets, skin on, pin bone removed

2 tablespoons canola oil

Kosher salt

Ground black pepper

½ cup walnut halves, reserve a few for garnish

1 large garlic clove, smashed

1 teaspoon coriander seeds

½ teaspoon kosher salt

1/8 teaspoon black pepper

2 cups fresh cilantro

¼ cup flat leaf parsley

2 teaspoons lemon juice

¼ cup olive oil, plus additional to cover the pesto

¼ cup shredded Parmesan cheese

Zest from ½ lemon (optional)

1. Preheat oven to 350 degrees.

2. Remove salmon from refrigerator. Rub canola oil on top and bottom of salmon. Sprinkle top with salt and pepper.

3. To prepare the pesto, spread walnuts on a baking sheet. Roast in preheat oven for 8 minutes. Remove from heat to cool.

4. Process walnuts, garlic, coriander, salt and pepper for about 30 seconds in a food processor. Scrape down sides and pulse 2 to 3 short bursts.

5. Add cilantro and parsley and pulse four to five bursts. While food processor is running, add lemon juice and oil until smooth 10 to 20 seconds.

6. Add processed cilantro walnut mix to a small bowl.

7. Add Parmesan cheese and stir.

8. Cover top of pesto with a thin layer of oil.

9. To prepare the salmon, heat a griddle on medium high heat for 3 to 4 minutes.

10. Reduce heat to medium and arrange the salmon on the griddle flesh-side down. Cook for 3 minutes, turn once and cook 3 to 4 minutes for medium.

11. Remove from heat. Arrange on a platter for family-style or individual plates. Plop a tablespoon of Cilantro Walnut Pesto on top. Garnish with reserved chopped walnuts.

ON THE GRILL

SALMON WITH PESTO AND GOAT CHEESE CRUMBLES **122** · GRILLED SALMON WITH ROASTED BEETS, BLUE CHEESE, AND PEAR VINAIGRETTE **125**

SALMON
WITH PESTO AND GOAT CHEESE CRUMBLES

SERVES 4-6

Certain foods are synonymous with summer. Salmon and basil are two of those foods. What better way to celebrate the bounty of summer than to marry the two with this super simple recipe. Add family, warm weather, sunshine, and summer's other favorite vegetables—tomatoes and corn on the cob—for a quick, easygoing weekend meal.

> **COOK'S NOTE**
>
> Pine nuts are the tradition nut of choice for pesto, but they are expensive. I make pesto with pecans, pistachios, and walnuts depending on what's stocked in my pantry (or on sale at the market). Each nut gives a distinct flavor and all complement the sweet, buttery flavor of salmon. Pour a layer of olive oil over unused pesto. Cover, refrigerate, and use within two days or freeze in small containers so you can enjoy this dish when fresh basil isn't available.

1/2 cup nuts (your choice)

2 garlic cloves, peeled

1/2 cup olive oil

3 cups fresh basil

1/2 cup Parmesan cheese, grated

Juice from 1/2 lemon

1 teaspoon kosher salt

Black pepper, to taste

1 to 1 1/2 pounds salmon fillet, skin on, cut into equal portions

Canola oil

Salt

Black pepper

4 ounces goat cheese

1. Add nuts and garlic to a food processor. Pulse four times or until nuts and garlic are ground.

2. Pour 1/4 cup of the olive oil into the food processor while blades spin.

3. Add basil. Pulse several times.

4. Add remaining olive oil until smooth.

5. Transfer mix to a medium bowl. Add Parmesan, lemon juice, salt, and pepper. Stir.

6. Heat a grill to medium. Oil the grill.

7. Rub the salmon portions with canola oil and sprinkle the tops with salt and pepper.

8. Place salmon on the grill skin-side down and cook for 3 minutes. Turn and cook another 3 to 4 minutes for medium, more or less depending on thickness and desired doneness.

9. Transfer to a platter. Spread a teaspoon of pesto on the hot salmon and top with crumbled goat cheese. Serve immediately.

GRILLED SALMON
WITH ROASTED BEETS, BLUE CHEESE, AND PEAR VINAIGRETTE

SERVES 4

The earthy flavors of beets and the tang of blue cheese are mellowed out by the sweetness of the salmon and the pear vinaigrette in this no-fuss midweek meal.

> **COOK'S NOTE** | To save time, roast beets ahead up to four days. Cover and refrigerate. Make the vinaigrette ahead one day, but don't add the oil until you're ready to serve. Don't slice pear until you are ready to serve, to avoid browning.

Vinaigrette
yield: 1/2 cup

1/2 cup pear juice

2 tablespoons champagne vinegar

1/2 teaspoon Dijon mustard

1/2 teaspoon dried tarragon

Vinaigrette (cont.)

Dash kosher salt

Dash black pepper

6 tablespoons olive oil

1 small head red leaf lettuce, washed

2 large or 4 small beets, roasted and quartered

1 celery stalk, cut on the bias, 1/4-inch thick

4 ounces blue cheese, crumbled

1/2 cup pecan halves

4 (4- to 6-ounce) salmon portions, skin on

Canola oil

Kosher salt

Black pepper

1 pear, sliced

1. To make the vinaigrette: Whisk pear juice, vinegar, mustard, tarragon, salt, and pepper in a small bowl. Drizzle the oil into the mix as you whisk to create a smooth emulsion.

2. Divide lettuce in four bowls or one large platter for family-style dining. Arrange beets, celery, blue cheese, and pecans around the outside of the lettuce, leaving the center for the salmon.

3. Heat a grill to medium heat and oil the grates.

4. Rub oil on salmon flesh and skin. Sprinkle the top of the salmon with salt and pepper.

5. Place salmon on the grill skin-side down. Cook 2 to 3 minutes. Resist the urge to move the salmon. Turn salmon top-side down

6. Arrange the sliced pear over the top of the salmon. Dress the salad with Pear Vinaigrette and serve immediately.

8

CHEF-INSPIRED RECIPES

Now that you have cooked a few of the Everyday Salmon Recipes, you are ready to venture into more challenging recipes. The following ten recipes were donated by chefs and organizations that support the sustainable seafood movement and ocean conservation.

As with all recipes, read the entire recipe before you begin to cook, create your *mise en place*, and buy the freshest, most sustainable salmon your budget allows to ensure a delicious meal every time.

FLORIDA SUNSHINE SALMON WITH AVOCADO MOUSSE, CITRUS SALSA, AND CILANTRO OIL 132 • BAKED SALMON WITH BOK CHOY AND GINGER 137 • GRILLED SALMON WITH CRACKED PEPPER AND BACON 140 • SALMON WITH ROASTED PEPPER, KALAMATA, AND RAISIN RELISH 142 • GRILLED SALMON WITH HOISIN GLAZE AND ASIAN SLAW 145 • ALASKA KING LOX 148 • BAKED SHIITAKE-TOMATO ATLANTIC SALMON 151 • BAKED ANCHO CHILE VERLASO SALMON CAKES WITH LEMON AND ROASTED GARLIC AIOLI 153 • ASIAN GLAZED GRILLED SALMON 157 • BROILED LEMON HERB SALMON 160

CHEF VICTORIA ALLMAN

FLORIDA SUNSHINE SALMON
WITH AVOCADO MOUSSE, CITRUS SALSA, AND CILANTRO OIL

SERVES 8

Victoria Allman is an international yacht chef and the author of Sea Fare: A Chef's Journey Across The Oceans and SEAsoned: A Chef's Journey with Her Captain. Victoria has a special fondness and appreciation of the oceans and sustainable seafood. Her fresh, elegant recipes reflect her travels and the local food found around the world. Enjoy this recipe created by Victoria with the flavors of the Sunshine State in mind.

COOK'S NOTE | The salmon in this recipe is served raw. Wear plastic disposable gloves when working with raw salmon and habanero peppers, which are the hottest peppers you'll find in the grocery store. The prepared salmon will keep under refrigeration for about six days.

Florida Sunshine Salmon

2 pounds chinook salmon fillet
1 cup kosher salt
1 cup sugar
1 teaspoon black pepper
1 orange, zested
1 lemon, zested
2 limes, zested
1/4 cup cilantro, chopped

Cilantro Oil

2 bunches cilantro
1 cup grapeseed oil

Avocado Mousse

2 avocadoes
1/4 cup plain Greek yogurt
1/2 teaspoon sea salt
1 lime, juiced

Citrus Salsa

	4 oranges, segmented
	2 tablespoons minced red onion
	2 tablespoons minced cilantro
	1/4 red habanero pepper, minced (or to heat tolerance)
	1/4 teaspoon sea salt
	Juice of 1 lime

To make the salmon:

1. Rinse the salmon under cold water.

2. Leave the skin on, but carefully remove bones from the salmon fillet with a pair of fish tweezers.

3. Mix together the salt, sugar, pepper, citrus zests, and cilantro in a large bowl.

4. Gently rub the seasonings onto the flesh of the fish and place inside a sealable plastic container with the seasoning mixture fully covering all sides of the fish.

5. Refrigerate for at least 24 hours.

To make the cilantro oil:

1. Blanche the cilantro in salted boiling water for 15 seconds.

2. Drain and immediately plunge the cilantro into ice water to retain a vivid green color.

3. Drain the ice water and gently squeeze out the excess water with a paper towel.

4. Place cilantro and oil in a blender. Purée for 1 minute to infuse the color and flavor into the oil.

5. Let sit for 4 hours and then strain through cheesecloth to remove the cilantro and leave a bright green oil.

To make the avocado mousse:

1. Mash the avocado, yogurt, sea salt, and lime juice together in a small bowl until smooth. Pass through a sieve to create a creamy smooth texture.

To make the citrus salsa:

1. Stir together oranges, onion, cilantro, chile, salt, and lime juice, and taste for seasoning as well as heat. Adjust with citrus juice if too hot.

To assemble:

1. Rinse the fish under cold water to remove the salt mixture.

2. Pat the fillet dry with paper towel.

3. Slice the fish on a 45-degree angle, wafer thin, away from the skin. Shingle layers of the salmon on the center of a large plate.

4. Place the avocado mousse in a piping bag and pipe over the center of the salmon for a pretty presentation, or spoon a

dollop in the center of the dish on top of the salmon.

5. Scoop a large spoon of citrus salsa over the avocado mousse and drizzle the cilantro oil around the plate.

TWIN MAPLES ORGANICS

BAKED SALMON
WITH BOK CHOY AND GINGER

SERVES 4

Chef Chris and Elizabeth Devoto are personal chef/owners of Twin Maples Organics, a 100-acre certified organic farm and CSA in western Kentucky. Advocates for all things sustainable and healthy, The Devoto's share their love for all things organic and Kentucky on their family homestead in Anton, KY. This simple, quick recipe embodies their down-to-earth lifestyle and mission.

4 (6-ounce) salmon fillets, skin on

4 tablespoons Asian chili sauce

2 tablespoons soy sauce

1 tablespoon finely grated ginger

2 tablespoons vegetable oil

1 tablespoon minced ginger

3 garlic cloves, minced

1 pound bok choy, quartered

8 ounces sugar snap peas, trimmed

1 tablespoon soy sauce

1 tablespoon rice wine vinegar

1 teaspoon sesame oil

Chives, if desired

To make the salmon:

1. Line a baking sheet with foil, and coat foil with an oil spray.
2. Whisk the chili sauce, soy sauce, and ginger and place in a bag large enough to fit the salmon.
3. Place salmon in the bag to marinate at room temperature for 30 minutes. Begin preheating the broiler.
4. Place salmon fillets skin-side down on prepared sheet.
5. Broil salmon without turning, until browned about 8 minutes, depending on thickness of salmon.

To make the bok choy:

1. Heat oil in a wok or heavy skillet over medium-high heat.
2. Add ginger and garlic. Stir about 30 seconds.
3. Add bok choy and sugar snap peas, and stir until crisp tender, about 4 minutes.
4. Add soy sauce and 1 vinegar, and combine. Heat 1 minute

longer. Finish with 1 teaspoon sesame oil.

5. Portion bok choy mixture onto the center of four plates, and place one salmon fillet on each plate. Garnish with chives.

CHEF RON DUPRAT

GRILLED SALMON
WITH CRACKED PEPPER AND BACON

SERVES 4

Ron Duprat is a celebrated Caribbean chef and food activist. His Haitian roots influence his cuisine, and his love for sustainable, local seafood is an inherent part of his life and career. His recipes are exotic, yet simple, like the recipe he shares here.

8 tablespoons (1 stick) unsalted butter

2 tablespoons whole black peppercorns

4 salmon steaks, approximately 8 ounces each

Salt

4 slices bacon, cut on the bias, into 1/4-inch pieces

4 lemon wedges for garnish

1. Preheat the broiler.

2. Clarify the butter: Melt butter in a small pan over low heat. Skim the froth of casein that rises to the surface, then spoon out the clear yellow liquid (clarified butter) without disturbing the layer of whey in the bottom of the pan. Save 1/4 cup of clarified butter for the salmon. Refrigerate any extra for another use.

3. Rock a heavy saucepan over the peppercorns to crack them.

4. Brush the salmon steaks with clarified butter. Season with salt and sprinkle them with the cracked pepper.

5. Broil under medium-high heat until half done (about 4 minutes).

6. Sprinkle bacon over each steak and continue cooking until the salmon flesh flakes easily from the center bone, about 4 minutes longer.

7. To serve, remove the central bone (actually part of the spine) and the large bones in the tail of the steak. Catch an edge of the skin with a fork and peel it off. Serve with lemon wedges.

CHEF NORA GALDIANO

SALMON
WITH ROASTED PEPPER, KALAMATA, AND RAISIN RELISH

SERVES 4

Nora Galdiano is a chef and culinary specialist for Sysco Central Florida. She is the Culinary Affairs Chairperson for the ACF Central Florida. I know how discriminating Nora is about the sustainable seafood—I sold her many a whole salmon! This native Hawaiian chef respects all things ocean- and seafood-related. She created this intense, lively sweet relish to complement the rich, bold flavor of salmon. Lemon-scented couscous makes a wonderful accompaniment.

> **COOK'S NOTE** | Make relish two to three hours in advance to allow all the flavors to develop together.

1 cup whole roasted red bell peppers, canned or jarred

1/4 cup kalamata olives, pitted, cut into quarters

1/4 cup golden raisins

1/4 cup diced red onions,

3 tablespoons olive oil

3 tablespoons chopped cilantro

2 tablespoons fresh lemon juice

1 tablespoon chopped mint,

1 teaspoon orange zest

1/4 teaspoon cayenne pepper

1/2 teaspoon cumin

1/4 teaspoon cinnamon

1/2 teaspoon kosher salt

4 (6-ounce salmon fillets), skin on

Salt and pepper

2 tablespoons olive oil

1. Drain water from the container of roasted red bell peppers and remove any seeds from the membranes that are intact.

2. Cut peppers into small dice and place in a large bowl.

3. Add the olives, raisins, red onions, olive oil, cilantro, lemon juice, mint, orange zest, cayenne, cumin, cinnamon, and salt to the bowl. Mix well.

4. Cover with plastic wrap and refrigerate until ready to use.

5. Heat a 12-inch skillet over medium heat.

6. While the pan heats, season the salmon fillets with salt and pepper.

7. Add olive oil to the pan, and swirl to coat. Place salmon fillets skin-side up in the pan.

8. Cook salmon about 3 to 4 minutes each side depending on preferred doneness.

9. Transfer salmon to plates. Scoop a spoonful of relish on top of each fillet. Serve immediately.

CHEF RICK MOONEN

GRILLED SALMON
WITH HOISIN GLAZE AND ASIAN SLAW

SERVES 4

Rick Moonen is an award-winning chef, educator, author, and leader in the sustainable seafood movement. He is a member of the Monterey Bay Aquarium Blue Ribbon Task Force. He is also the celebrated chef-owner of RM Seafood in Las Vegas. Rick creates approachable, classic, and contemporary dishes like this recipe, a fast weeknight supper when you prepare it on a Foreman grill. Rick used True North Salmon for this recipe. You may also sub dorade, char, or rainbow trout, all sustainable seafood species.

Hoisin Glaze
yield: 1/4 cup

2 tablespoons hoisin sauce

Juice of 1/2 lime

1 teaspoon honey

1 small garlic clove, minced or put through a press

1 tablespoon minced fresh cilantro

Kosher salt

Asian Slaw	1 pound cabbage, cored and shredded
	1 cup grated carrots (use the large holes of a box grater or the shredding disk of a food processor)
	1/2 cup Asian Vinaigrette
	2 tablespoons chopped fresh mint
	Kosher salt
Grilled Salmon	4 (6- to 7-ounce) salmon fillets, skin on
	Kosher salt and freshly ground white pepper
	Olive oil

1. To make the glaze: Stir the hoisin, lime juice, honey, garlic, and cilantro together in a small bowl. Season with salt. This can sit on the counter for a couple of hours, or store covered in the refrigerator for up to 3 days.

2. To make the slaw: Toss the cabbage and carrots with the vinaigrette and mint in a medium bowl. Season with salt, toss, and taste. Adjust the salt if necessary. Cover with plastic wrap and refrigerate for 1 hour before serving.

3. Season the fish with salt and white pepper and coat each fillet with oil. You can prep this several hours in advance and keep it cold in the refrigerator.

4. Grill the salmon on a Foreman grill for 3 to 4 minutes. Give the fish a poke—it will feel firm when it's cooked. If using a cast-iron grill pan, grill the fillets for 1 1/2 minutes on the skin side, then turn and grill for another 1 1/2 minutes or until done. Alternatively, prepare a charcoal grill. When the coals are hot, set the grate on the lowest level (closest to the coals) and get it very hot. Brush the grate with vegetable oil. Grill the fillets for 1 1/2 minutes on the skin side, then turn and grill for another 1 to 1 1/2 minutes, until the fish feels firm.

5. When the fish is done, remove from the grill and brush the skin side with Hoisin Glaze. Serve immediately with a side of Asian Slaw.

MARTIN REED

ALASKA KING LOX

Martin Reed is the CEO of San Francisco–based Blue Sea Labs, a company dedicated to providing efficient, environmentally responsible solutions for food supply chains that support producers and consumers. His newest project, Two Fish, brings super fresh sustainable sushi direct from the boat to the market.

> **COOK'S NOTE** | The salmon in this recipe needs to cure for two to three days, so be sure to plan ahead. Buy the freshest cut of salmon available. I like king because it's fattier and doesn't have as strong a flavor as other types, such as sockeye. Keep in mind that if fish is frozen soon after catch, the quality is often much higher. Most people will tell you that you ought to freeze the salmon first anyway, since you won't be cooking it and these fish are susceptible to parasites.

1 cup salt

1 1/2 cups sugar

2 cups basil

1 lemon, zested

2 pounds of salmon, skin removed

1. Mix salt and sugar in a medium bowl.

2. Add basil and lemon zest. Stir.

3. Place salmon on plastic wrap and cover with salt and sugar mixture.

4. Wrap salmon in plastic wrap, leaving one end of the wrapped salmon open to drain juices.

5. Place wrapped fish on a tray or in a dish and prop one side higher than the other so that juices can drain out as they are pulled from the fish by the salt and sugar. Use crumpled foil to prop up the fish.

6. Place a heavy object (such as a foil-wrapped brick or cast-iron grill press) on top of the salmon and place the tray in the refrigerator. Store in the refrigerator for 2 or 3 days.

7. After 2 or 3 days, remove salmon, rinse, and pat dry.

8. Cut very thin slices along the side of the fillet.

9. Serve immediately or portion and freeze.

Serving suggestion: Top a bagel with cream cheese, capers, and cracked red pepper. Add salmon lox slices and a squeeze of fresh lemon or key lime.

TRUE NORTH SALMON COMPANY

BAKED SHIITAKE-TOMATO ATLANTIC SALMON

SERVES 4

True North Salmon Company is the largest BAP-certified, sustainable, farmed salmon company in North America. Established in 1985, it began with one marine cage and five thousand fish. Today, TNS is a family-run, premier company producing and supplying naturally raised, hormone-free fresh salmon in all forms—pre-seasoned salmon, all natural, hot and cold smoked salmon—to supermarkets and restaurants across North America.

4 (4- to 6-ounce) salmon portions, skin on

Salt and pepper

2 large shiitake mushrooms, stemmed and thinly sliced

1/2 cup chopped seeded tomatoes

2 green onions, chopped

2 teaspoons chopped fresh ginger

2 garlic cloves, minced

4 teaspoons soy sauce

2 teaspoons sesame oil

Fresh cilantro sprigs

1. Heat oven to 400 degrees.

2. Place the salmon, skin-side down, on a parchment-lined baking sheet. Season fillets with salt and pepper.

3. Place mushrooms, tomatoes, green onions, ginger, and garlic in a medium bowl, and stir.

4. Spread mixture over salmon fillets. Drizzle with soy sauce and sesame oil, then top with cilantro sprigs.

5. Bake for 8 to 10 minutes per inch of thickness. Serve immediately.

VERLASSO SALMON

BAKED ANCHO CHILE VERLASSO SALMON CAKES
WITH LEMON AND ROASTED GARLIC AIOLI

SERVES 6

Verlasso Salmon is the first farmed salmon company to get a "good alternative" rating on Seafood Watch. Dedicated to the environment and local workplace, its vision works in harmony with the pristine surrounding in Patagonia, Chile. This recipe is the perfect way to use leftover cooked salmon. Serve grilled salmon fillets the first night and salmon cakes the next night. When the oven is hot, the grill is fired up, or the burner is on, make a little extra. Leftovers can be used for a quick lunch or dinner the next day, saving you time and cooking energy.

Lemon and Roasted Garlic Aioli

1 full head of garlic

1 teaspoon olive oil

1 cup mayonnaise

2 tablespoons minced Italian parsley

2 teaspoons fresh lemon juice

Salmon Cakes

2 1/2 cups cooked Verlasso salmon fillet, loosely packed

1/2 cup panko bread crumbs or cracker crumbs

1/4 cup minced celery

1/4 cup minced green onion

1/4 cup mayonnaise

1 large egg

3 tablespoons chopped curly parsley

1 tablespoon Dijon mustard

1 tablespoon Worcestershire sauce

1 tablespoon ancho chile powder

Kosher salt and freshly ground pepper

Flour for dredging

Salmon Cakes (cont.)

1 tablespoon olive oil

---

1 tablespoon unsalted butter

To make the aioli:

1. Preheat oven to 425 degrees.

2. To prepare the aioli, cut 1/3 off the top of the garlic bulb. Place on a 6-by-6-inch piece of heavy-duty aluminum foil. Drizzle with olive oil.

3. Gather the foil and wrap around the garlic. Place in the oven and bake for 1 hour or until the garlic is soft and golden. Remove from the oven and let cool completely.

4. Gently press the garlic out of the garlic paper with your fingers or the flat side of a knife. With a knife, mash 1 tablespoon of the garlic. Reserve the remainder for another use.

5. In a small bowl, mix together mayonnaise, parsley, and lemon juice. Fold in the roasted garlic. Cover and refrigerate aioli for up to 5 days.

To make the salmon cakes:

1. In a large bowl, break the salmon fillets into small flakes. Add breadcrumbs, celery, green onion, mayonnaise, egg, parsley, Dijon, Worcestershire, and chili powder. Season with salt and pepper. Mix well, but gently.

2. Form the salmon mixture into 8 flat cakes or patties. Place flour in a shallow dish and dust each salmon cake lightly.

3. Lower the oven temperature to 400 degrees.

4. Heat the oil and butter in a large heavy skillet. Pan-fry the cakes for 2 to 3 minutes per side, until golden brown, turning very carefully so they do not fall apart. Place on a baking sheet.

5. Place the salmon cakes in the oven and bake for 10 minutes until cooked through and hot in the center.

6. Serve warm with Lemon and Roasted Garlic Aioli on the side.

MasterChef Junior
ALEXANDER WEISS

ASIAN GLAZED GRILLED SALMON

SERVES 4

Alexander Weiss took *MasterChef Junior* by storm in its first season, wowing the judges with his pistachio macaroons, charm, and fun attitude. This mature 13-year-old made his debut at the 2014 Monterey Bay Aquariums Cooking for Solutions event. His enthusiasm for all things food and his dedication to sustainable seafood is inspirational and exciting. Alex balances home life and high school with travel to Indonesia, Chicago, Los Angeles, and more while he creates easy-to-prepare recipes like his version of Asian Salmon.

> **COOK'S NOTE** | For the best flavor, allow the salmon to marinate overnight. Serve over soba noodles or rice with a light citrus vinaigrette.

Marinade

- 1/3 cup soy sauce
- 2 tablespoons dark brown sugar
- 2 1/2 tablespoons hoisin sauce

Marinade (cont.)

3 tablespoons grated fresh ginger

Red pepper flakes

2 garlic cloves, minced

2 tablespoons lime juice

2 lime leaves, crushed

2 tablespoons olive oil

A drop of rice wine vinegar or cider vinegar

1/2 tablespoon chili paste

1 tablespoon miso or yuzu paste, if desired

2 (4-ounce) salmon fillets, skin removed

Olive oil for grilling

Sliced green onions, for garnish

1. Mix together soy sauce, brown sugar, hoisin, ginger, red pepper, garlic, lime juice, lime leaves, oil, vinegar, chili paste, and miso in a medium bowl.

2. Put the salmon fillets in the bowl with the marinade, cover tightly with plastic wrap, and marinate in the refrigerator overnight.

3. Heat a grill or pan over medium heat.

4. Oil the hot grill generously and place the salmon fillets on top. Reserve the marinade.

5. Cook the salmon, watching closely, for 4 minutes per side. Do not touch the salmon while cooking. Flip only once.

6. Remove salmon from the grill and allow to rest for 5 minutes.

7. While salmon rests, simmer the marinade for 5 minutes.

8. Serve salmon with the sauce, and garnish with sliced green onions.

CHEF VIRGINIA WILLIS

BROILED LEMON HERB SALMON

SERVES 6

Virginia Willis is a Southern chef, TV personality, and author of the *Y'all* cookbook series. Her cooking style marries down-home comfort with a French twist. She is a member of the Monterey Bay Aquarium Blue Ribbon Task Force. Virginia cooked up this simple, yet elegant salmon recipe using Copper River salmon. Virginia's forthcoming TV series, "Secrets of the Southern Table: A Food Lovers Tour of the Global South" is currently in development for PBS.

1 large Copper River salmon fillet (about 1 1/2 pounds), scaled, with skin and pin bones removed
3 garlic cloves, very finely chopped
3 tablespoons dark brown sugar
3 tablespoons tamari, preferably wheat-free
6 tablespoons finely chopped fresh herbs, such as parsley, thyme, cilantro, and chives
3 tablespoons sesame oil

1/4 cup extra virgin olive oil

Zest and juice of 1 lemon

1 sweet onion, preferably Vidalia, thinly sliced

Kosher salt and freshly ground black pepper

1. Place the salmon in a shallow ovenproof baking dish or rimmed half sheet pan.

2. Combine the garlic, brown sugar, tamari, herbs, sesame oil, olive oil, lemon zest, and lemon juice in a bowl. Stir to combine and pour over salmon. Turn to coat.

3. Cover and refrigerate to marinate, 30 minutes to 1 hour. About 15 minutes before ready to cook, remove the salmon to the counter to come to room temperature.

4. Place oven rack about four inches from the heat source. Heat the oven to broil.

5. Sprinkle sliced onions over the top of the salmon.

6. Broil to medium rare, 5 to 7 minutes, depending on the strength of your broiler. Serve immediately.

ACKNOWLEDGEMENTS

Huge heartfelt thanks to the chefs in Chapter 8 Chef Inspired Recipes for their unwavering generosity and support. And to the Monterey Bay Aquarium for inviting me to the Sustainable Seafood Institute in 2013 where the seeds of this cookbook series sprouted.

Gratitude to the organizations and companies that donated salmon for the recipe development: Alaska Seafood Marketing Institute, CaughtWild Salmon, Copper River/Prince Williams Sound, and Verlasso Salmon. Thank you! All of these organizations and people are my heroes and inspiration for their continued dedication to the health of our oceans, marine conservation, sustainable fisheries, and the health of the planet.

This book would not be possible without my mother, Margaret Cavanaugh (1925–2000). She insisted that I make something out of my life other than being a wife and mom, which is what she wanted also. She gave me hope and courage to become the woman I am today. She taught me to believe in myself and to persevere, despite the nearly insurmountable challenges she knew would lie ahead. She'd be proud to know not only did I manage to get the married part right, but I created a lifestyle that involves the health of our oceans.

Thanks to Stephan C. Ban (1933–2013), Eva Ban, Vicki Platt, Lisa Murphy, Jane Wapner, Loryn McDonald, (1944-2015), Patti Tryba, Lucy Reynolds, Cookie, and all the other servers, cooks, and kitchen staff at The Wooden Spoon Restaurant where my culinary adventure began in

1989. More important though, a heartfelt shout out to my loyal friends and customers who kept me company, listened to my stories, and loved my cooking for ten years.

Special thanks to Rachel Duchak (Central Coast Foodie), Gina Murphy-Darling (Mrs. Greens World), and Minako IUE (Sailors for the Sea Japan), SFI friends for life.

Another big shout out to the chefs, fishermen, seafood suppliers, corporations, dock managers, and friends in the wholesale seafood distribution industry, the restaurant industry, and fishing community. Thank you for protecting the oceans and creating sustainable fisheries for the future.

Special thanks to friends Wendy Chasser, Tori Eurton, Pamela McColloch, Carey Ann Weiss, Donna Fitzgerald, Erich Steinbock, Elizabeth Fortescue, Cody Allison, Ann Gipson, Mary Zimmer, Stephanie Thomas Taylor, Beth Woods, Taylor Riley, and Joel Meador.

Thanks to Margaret Sutherland, Jennifer Travis, Deborah Balmuth, Susan Spann, Katherine Pickett, Jamie Morris, Mary Ann de Stefano, Dianne Jacob and Danielle Svetcov.

Thanks to my family in Pennsylvania and Kentucky for your encouragement and love.

I invite you to share your thoughts, ideas, and reviews about *Salmon* on Amazon, Twitter, Facebook, Pinterest, Instagram, Goodreads, and on my website **www.maureencberry.com**. For more information about sustainable seafood news and easy-to-prepare seafood recipes, feel free to email me, or tweet me **@maureencberry** . Thank you for buying *Salmon*. Make sure you stay connected for news about my projects and the next book in the sustainable seafood cookbook series, *Shrimp*.

Lastly, this book would not be possible without the everlasting love, encouragement and support from my husband, Larry. He is my anchor when I flounder around without direction or conviction.

M

SHOPPING FOR SALMON

- Alaska Seafood Marketing Institute (ASMI): 800-478-2903; **www.alaskaseafood.org**

- Caught Wild: 859-247-0579; **www.CaughtWildSalmon.com**

- Copper River Seafood: 907-865-5033; **www.copperriverseafoods.com**

- Local Catch (CSF): **www.localcatch.org/locator/**

- Northwest Atlantic Marine Alliance(CSF): **www.namanet.org/csf**

- Seafood Watch: **www.montereybayaquarium.org/conservation/research/seafood-watch**

True North Salmon Company: 877-407-5577;
www.truenorthsalmon.com

Two Fish: **www.gettwofish.com**

Verlasso Salmon: **www.verlasso.com**

Vital Choice: 800-608 4825;
www.vitalchoice.com/shop/pc/home.asp

SUSTAINABLE ORGANIZATIONS AND RESOURCES

 Aurora Algae: 510-266-5001; **www.aurorainc.com**

 Best Practices Aquaculture (BAP): 314-293-5500; **www.bestaquaculturepractices.org**

 Bristol Bay Regional Development Association: 206-491-6829; **www.bristolbaysockeye.org**

 Conservation Alliance for Seafood Solutions: **www.solutionsforseafood.org**

 Copper River/ Prince William Sound Marketing Association: 907-424-3459; **www.soundsalmon.org**

 Environmental Defense Fund: **www.edf.org**

EWOS: +47-55-69-70-00 (Norway); **www.ewos.com**

Fycology: **www.fycology.com**

Global Aquaculture Alliance (GAA): 314-293-5500; **www.gaalliance.org**

Magnuson-Stevens Fisheries Conservation and Management Act: **www.nmfs.noaa.gov/sfa/magact/**

Marine Stewardship Council (MSC): 206-691-0188; **www.msc.org**

Monterey Bay Aquarium Seafood Watch: 831-648-4800; **www.seafoodwatch.org/**

National Geographic: 800-647-5463; **www.ocean.nationalgeographic.com/ocean/**

NOAA: **www.oceanservice.noaa.gov/**

Oceana: **www.oceana.org/en**

Sea Choice: 604-696-5400; **www.seachoice.org/**

Seafood Choices Alliance: **www.seafoodwatch.org/**

 The Safina Center (formerly Blue Ocean Institute): 631-632-3763; **www.safinacenter.org**

 World Wildlife Fund (WWF): **www.wwf.panda.org/**

CONTRIBUTING CHEFS AND CORPORATIONS

- Chef Victoria Allman; **www.victoriaallman.com/**

- Chef Chris Devoto; **twinmaplesorganics@gmail.com**

- Chef Ron Duprat; **www.amazon.com/My-Journey-Cooking-Ron-Duprat/dp/1434333752**

- Chef Nora Galdiano; **www.linkedin.com/in/noragaldiano**

- Chef Rick Moonen; **www.rickmoonen.com/**

- Martin Reed; **www.bluesealabs.com/**

- True North Salmon Company; **www.truenorthsalmon.com/**

🐟 Verlasso Salmon; **www.verlasso.com/**

🐟 MasterChef Junior Alexander Weiss; **www.masterchef-junior.wikia.com/wiki/Alexander**

🐟 Chef Virginia Willis; **www.virginiawillis.com/**

CONTRIBUTORS

INDEX

Alaska, 4-5, 9, 12-15, 24, 32, 34, 53, 77-83, 148-150, 165, 168

Alaska Seafood Marketing Institute (ASMI), 15, 34, 165, 168

Albumin, 52-53

Aquabounty Technologies, 30

Aquaculture, 4-5, 8 19, 21-25, 29, 170-171

AquAdvantage salmon, 30

Best Aquatic Practice (BAP), 7, 15, 22-23, 25, 29, 34, 151, 170

Buying salmon

    At the market, 28-35

    Farmed, 19, 28-30

    Fresh, 30-32

    Frozen, 34

    Online, 34

    Wild, 13-15, 30-32

Bycatch, 5-6, 35

CaughtWild Salmon, 77-79, 165, 168

Certify, 7

Chef recipes

        Allman, Chef Victoria, Florida Sunshine Salmon with Avocado Mousse, Citrus Salsa, and Cilantro Oil, 132-136

        Devoto, Chris and Elizabeth, Organics Chefs, Baked Salmon with Bok Choy and Ginger, 137-139

Duprat, Chef Ron, Grilled Salmon with Cracked Pepper and Bacon, 140-141

Galdiano, Chef Nora, Salmon with Roasted Pepper, Kalamata, and Raisin Relish, 142-144

Moonen, Chef Rick, Grilled Salmon with Hoisin Glaze and Asian Slaw, 145-147

Reed, Martin, Blue Sea Labs, Alaska King Lox, 148-150

True North Salmon Company, Baked Shiitake-Tomato Atlantic Salmon, 151-152

Verlasso Salmon, Baked Ancho Chile Verlasso Salmon Cakes with Lemon and Roasted Garlic Aioli, 153-156

Weiss, Alexander, MasterChef Junior, Asian Glazed Grilled Salmon, 157-159

Willis, Chef Virginia, Broiled Lemon Herb Salmon, 160-161

Citrus, 39-40, 59-63, 67-85, 90-92, 101-108, 112-118, 122-124, 131-136, 140-150, 153-161

Color, salmon, 13-15, 19, 31

Commodity, 183

Community Supported Fishery (CSF), 6, 34-35, 168

Conserve, or conservation, 2-9, 22, 28, 130, 165, 183

Cooking

    Methods, 53-54

    Techniques, 53-54

    Temperature, 52

    Time, 52-53

    Tips, 52-55

Copper River/Prince Williams Sound, 112-115, 165, 170

Country of origin, 28

Eco-labels, 8

Escapement, 23, 30

Farmed salmon
    About, 17-25
    Buying, 19, 28-30
    Caring for, 21-22
    Fresh, 30-32
    Frozen, 34

FDA, 30

Fishermen, 4-6, 21, 28, 35

Fish feed, 8, 19, 21-23, 25

Florida, 24, 131-136, 142

Genetically modified salmon, 30

Global Aquaculture Alliance (GAA), 23, 29, 171

Grill, 54, 121-127, 140-141, 145-147, 157-159,

Guides for sustainable salmon and seafood, 14, 19

Harvested, 3, 5, 8, 13

Healthy properties, 8-9, 22, 24-25, 50

Herbs, list of, 40

Kitchen
    Timer, 45, 50, 52, 54
    Tools, 42-47, 50

Knives, 43-45

Marine Stewardship Council (MSC), 7, 15, 22-23, 29, 34, 171, 181

Monterey Bay Aquarium, 6, 22, 28, 145, 160, 165, 171, 181

Oils, 14-15, 21-22, 38-39, 41, 53-55

Oven, cooking, 47, 53-55, 59-83

National Oceanic and Atmospheric Administration (NOAA), 3-4, 6, 12, 171

Nutritional, 50

Nuts, 41, 45, 59-63, 69-75, 85, 116-118, 121-127

Ocean pens, 19, 23-24, 30

Oceans, 3-9, 12-13, 21-25, 28, 30-31, 35, 132, 165-166

Omega-3, or Omega-3s, 9, 22, 50-51

Pantry, 40-42

Resources, 168-74

Salads, 61-63, 72-75, 87-89, 125-127

Salmon

    Alaska, 4, 9, 12-15, 24, 32, 34, 53-54, 77-79, 80-83, 148-150

    Farmed, 4, 7-9, 17-25, 28-30

    GMO, 30

    North Atlantic, 12, 151-152, 168

    Pacific, 12-13

    Recipes

        Alaska King Lox, Blue Sea Labs Martin Reed, 148-150

        Asian Glazed Grilled Salmon, MasterChef Junior Alexander Weiss, 157-159

        Baked Ancho Chile Verlasso Salmon Cakes with Lemon and Roasted Garlic Aioli Verlasso Salmon, 153-156

        Broiled Lemon Herb Salmon Chef Virginia Willis, 160-161

        Baked Salmon with Bok Choy and Ginger Organics Chefs Chris and Elizabeth Devoto, 137-139

        Baked Shiitake-Tomato Atlantic Salmon True North Salmon Company, 151-152

        Cumin-Dusted Salmon Bowl with Peanut-Thai Slaw, 72-75

        Farmers Market Salmon Salad, 86-89

        Florida Sunshine Salmon with Avocado Mousse, Citrus Salsa, and Cilantro Oil Chef Victoria Allman, 132-136

        Grilled Salmon with Roasted Beets, Blue Cheese, and Pear Vinaigrette, 125-127

Grilled Salmon with Cracked Pepper and Bacon Chef Ron Duprat, 140-141

Grilled Salmon with Hoisin Glaze and Asian Slaw Chef Rick Moonen, 145-147

Honey Mustard Salmon with Very Berry Vinaigrette, 64-66

Mediterranean Salmon with Chickpea Mash, 106-108

Pan-Grilled Salmon with Cilantro-Walnut Pesto, 116-118

Poached Salmon with Cheese Grits and Eggs, 96-98

Salmon Burger with Cranberry Yogurt, 112-115

Salmon Corn Chowder, 109-111

Salmon Flatbread with Mandarin Orange and Fennel, 67-68

Salmon in Parchment, 80-83

Salmon with Orange-Bourbon Glaze, 101-103

Salmon with Pesto and Goat Cheese Crumbles, 122-124

Salmon with Roasted Apples and Walnuts, 69-71

Salmon with Roasted Pepper, Kalamata, and Raisin Relish Chef Nora Galdiano, 142-144

Salmon with Spicy Peach Salsa, 90-92

Simple Steamed Salmon, 104-105

Slow-Roasted Salmon Salad: Three Ways, 60-63

Slow Roasted Salmon with Blueberry Pan Sauce, 76-79

Spicy Salmon Rice Bowl, 99-100

Summer Salmon Chowder, 93-95

Wild, 4-5, 8-9, 11-15, 30-33

Salt, 38-40, 53, 55

Sauces, 41, 77-79, 80-83, 99-100

Sea Choice, 3-4, 171

Seafood specialist

Seafood Watch, 6-7, 22, 28, 153, 168, 171

Shopping, for salmon, 27-35, 168-169

Skillets, 45-47, 54

Spices, 40

Stovetop, 43, 45, 47, 54-55, 85-119

Sustainable
- Definition, 3-4
- Oceans, 6-9, 22-23, 28, 34-35
- Salmon, 1-9, 15, 25, 28-30, 34-35
- Seafood, 1-9, 15, 25, 28-30, 34-35

Tips
- Fish, 30-35, 53-55
- Cooking, 53-55
- Shopping, 30-35, 46-47

Traceability, 6, 23, 25, 28

True North Salmon, 22, 145-147, 151-52, 169, 173

Verlasso, 22, 25, 153-56, 165, 169, 174

Wild salmon
- About, 12-13
- Buying, 13-15
- Caring for
- Fresh, 30-32
- Frozen, 32-33
- Seasons, 13, 35
- Types, 13-15

Websites for sustainable resources, shopping, 168-72

Wholesale distribution, 6, 24, 166

Wine, cooking with, 39

World Wildlife Fund (WWF), 19-21, 50, 172

ABOUT THE AUTHOR

Maureen C. Berry has worked in the food industry since 1989 as a restauranteur, sales representative, and commodity seafood buyer. She has written for *Edible Orlando* magazine and blogs at *Conservation: tackling sustainable news (formerly Seafood Lady)*. She attends the annual Monterey Bay Aquarium's Sustainable Foods Institute, collaborates with Marine Stewardship Council, The Sustainable Seafood Blog Project, Fish 2.0, and American Shrimp Processors Association. She believes that our choices make a difference, and that what we do on land has a direct effect on our oceans and planet.

Maureen lives in Kentucky with her husband and their feisty wire fox terrier. When she is not baking buttermilk biscuits, photographing wildlife in her woods, or taking naps, she is researching and cooking for her next cookbook in the series. You can find her tweeting **@maureencberry**. This is her first book.

Please visit **www.maureencberry.com**

www.ingramcontent.com/pod-product-compliance
Lightning Source LLC
Chambersburg PA
CBHW040333300426
44113CB00021B/2744